PETER O'TOOLE

PETER O'TOOLE

a biography by
Michael Freedland

ST. MARTIN'S PRESS
NEW YORK

First Edition
10 9 8 7 6 5 4 3 2 1

FOR SYLVIA

The Godmother, with love

Acknowledgements

PETER O'TOOLE'S CAREER is not the easiest to write about. No actor can be who defies convention and almost literally becomes an overnight sensation. But then his is not an ordinary life.

If he didn't do much in the way of suffering in garrets to start with, the sheer brilliance of an actor who can be spotted as a genius at his first audition singles him out as someone special. The past twenty years have proved just how special he is. Perhaps the greatest actor of his generation; the only performer who can hit the front pages of newspapers all over the world with the effects of his interpretation of a play by Shakespeare. A man whose roustabout exploits vie with those of an Errol Flynn or a John Barrymore.

At fifty years old, O'Toole still has a number of years at the top of his profession in front of him. But it is already easy to say we shall not see his like again. A number of people have helped me put this fact into focus. Some of them, for reasons I respect, have not wanted me to quote them by name. But to them, and to these kind men and women—many at the top of their professions in the world of theatre and cinema—who have granted me interviews, my sincerest thanks:

Ernie Anderson, April Ashley, George Baker, John Barton, Nat Brenner, Michael Bryant, John Coe, Shirley Dixon, Frank Finlay, Robert Ginna, Jack Gold, Sir Peter Hall, John Huston, Frank Kelly, Roy Kinnear, James Mason, John Le Mesurier, Val May, Andrew Leigh, Joseph O'Connor, Donald Pleasence, Malcolm Rogers, Robert

Rietty, Elizabeth Sellars, Nigel Stock, J. Lee Thompson, John Thompson, James Villiers, Hal B. Wallis, Judy Wilson, Peter Yates. Additional thanks for their kind help to David Nathan, Peter Noble, and Barbara Paskin.

And for her very great assistance through much of the preparation of this book, Sylvia Mindel. Also my sincerest thanks to the staff of the Theatre Royal, Bristol, the Old Vic, London, the Royal Academy of Dramatic Art and the librarians of the British Film Institute, the British Library, and the *Daily Express,* London.

My thanks, too, to my editor, Amanda Girling. Finally, to my dearest wife, Sara, without whose patience this would never have materialised, my devotion.

Michael Freedland
London, 1982

One

IT IS NOT difficult to understand why, in the days when Hollywood had a sentimental streak, it made films in Connemara. Everything about it seemed to symbolise what Americans regarded as typically Irish. You only had to walk across the road in the village of Clifden to feel sure that before long a tiny bow-legged fiddler would be on your tail, leading the locals in a jig. And if you didn't actually spot any of the Little People in the course of your journey, you would have to accept that the reason was simply that they didn't often appear for strangers. You couldn't but believe that they were there.

It was—and is—one of the most beautiful places of God's earth. The sea, a defiant shade of blue, despite the frequent grey skies, laps a series of rocks and coves which seem to have been created simply to help artists get their canvases covered in paint without the effort of having to use too much imagination. You couldn't, in truth, imagine anything more enticing. The fields are as green as an Irish Government travel poster. The mountains rise high into the clouds and on their slopes graze the sheep and cows which for generations have given the locals their livelihood.

It is also horse territory. The distinctive Connemara ponies roam the byways and the streets at will, and although they were heard to make something of a fuss in 1919 when Messrs Alcock and Brown flew into their lives at the end of their celebrated transatlantic crossing, they leave the people alone and, in return, few of the people bother them either.

Horses of a different breed played a large part in the life of one of its leading citizens, Patrick Joseph O'Toole, known in every racecourse south of Ulster as 'the Captain' and occasionally Spats. The first title was the product of Patrick's own fertile thought processes; the second owed more to fact. It was an odds-on certainty that he would never appear at the track without this form of decoration on his shiny brown shoes. They were as regular an accessory to his person as the best quality broadcloth suiting he wore on his back, and the blackboard on which he recorded the terms for accepting the bets of the day's punters.

Patrick—inevitably, certain less respectful citizens called him Patty—was one of the most popular bookmakers for miles around, although for years he would list himself in the local telephone directory as a 'financial consultant'. It was a trade that Patrick had imbibed when other children were learning nursery rhymes. His mother was a distinguished member of the same profession—hiding her bookmaking activities behind the façade of a furniture shop.

Patty was powerfully built and fleet of foot, two characteristics that were to prove immensely important in his chosen occupation. When he met, and before long married, the beautiful Constance Ferguson, he was a happy man revelling in that popularity. His wife, the existence he had made for himself which enabled him to take full advantage of his gregarious personality and, above all, his deep, instinctive Irishness, made him a man who knew exactly what he wanted out of life. That name O'Toole was sufficient to implant a seed of Irish pride deep inside him. When the O'Tooles' daughter was born, it seemed only right to call her after the country's patron saint, too—to say nothing of her father. She became Patricia. Then when the O'Tooles' son was born on 2 August 1932, a full decade after the establishment of the Irish Free State, it was taken for granted that he, too, would have to have an Irish name. So they called him Peter Seamus O'Toole. If the first name gave no indication of his origins, Seamus left no room at all for doubt.

The O'Tooles, the ones from which he had been descended, were the ancient kings of Ireland and had lived in Connemara themselves in the days when Dublin was a mere track of wasteland on the other side of the country. More than that, Connemara was part of County Galway and a stone's throw from Galway itself, a town which meant more to the people living in the area than could ever be conveyed in a line from a Bing Crosby song. To them, it was the centre of chivalry, Irish style—a fact that brought Patrick a great sense of pride. He knew that he was one of the aristocracy.

The way he carried out his 'profession' was part of a personality that stemmed from a background with which not everyone had been blessed.

'He was a bookie, not a turf accountant,' his son was to recall. 'In the Silver Ring, in the twenties, you didn't have a clientele, you had to drum it up.'

Before long, the family had crossed the Irish Sea and set up home first in Gainsborough in Lincolnshire and then in Leeds, and it was there and not in Ireland that Peter's formative years were spent; in a tiny back-to-back terraced house in Burton Street, Hunslet. The house cost a few shillings to rent, but the O'Tooles left no one in doubt that they considered it to be the residence-in-exile of members of the Irish blood royal. The 'Captain's' business activities continued from there, too.

Connie probably helped him in that regard. She was as much an extrovert as her husband and was not beyond kicking up her legs in public in a riotous dance of the time. Her son's future career owes not a little to that background.

The 'Captain' was not always a great financial success. On the course, he tended to confuse the odds rather more frequently than was generally considered to be sound and when that happened, the dust left by his trail seemed to choke more people than that thrown up by the cantering horses on a different part of the track. When Peter was old enough to join 'the Captain' on these expeditions to the racecourse, he knew the drill well enough. At a given signal from his

11

father—bookies were extraordinarily adept at conveying a wealth of information with a wink, a nod or an inflection of the fingers—Peter would help him pack his brown leather bag and escape into a nearby hedge, with the command from Patty: 'Come on, son, let's be off.'

Years later, Peter would deny that he came from a working-class background. 'I come straight from the criminal classes,' he maintained—although a glass too many of Guinness or Irish whiskey was about as far as Patty's criminal activities went. His escapes from the spot where the punters had made their investments was undoubtedly his most serious misdemeanour.

Peter's grandmother had by then set up shop in Leeds, too, running, once more, her furniture business as the front for her betting activities—a highly illegal arrangement. There were times when he spent more time with her than he did with the 'Captain'. With her he got to know some of the choicest racing territory in the country. The racecourses of the Yorkshire dales have become part of the O'Toole heritage. So, for many years, had Hunslet. He was still playing rugby for the local team when he had long moved from the area and was already a leading actor.

Peter learned to read at three. By the time he was four, he was devouring stories of the knights in armour who had left Galway long before any part of the ould sod had been trampled down to make way for a racetrack—a fact that pleased Patrick and Constance no little bit.

At St Anne's, the local Catholic school—'Christ, was it Catholic!' he has since said—Peter allowed the romance of those stories to envelop him, much to the dismay of the priests and the nuns who were his first teachers. It was also the time when he brushed with authority for the first time. How much of his attitude at this stage of his life was due to parental, iconoclastic influence or simply to an inbred desire to be an exhibitionist can only be guessed at—although few psychiatrists would disagree that what went on in and around Burton Street must have had something to do with it.

It could also have been partly due to the fact that he was left-handed, a state of affairs that the nuns at the school found difficult to accept. They seemed to regard a child's inability to use his right hand as well as his left as a sickness or a curse. Either way, it was a condition that had to be rectified.

Their solution to the 'problem' was to force their pupils to write, pick up, or work things only with their right hands. If Peter or any of his fellow left-handed pupils failed to benefit from this method—bred from generations of experience in the convents of Ireland—the treatment was simply a near-karate chop with a ruler over the knuckles.

In his more reflective moments, Peter O'Toole has claimed that the numerous injuries, breaks, strains and bruises he has since suffered to his right hand were simply his way of showing his resentment of those nuns; a kind of masochistic revenge. His right hand bears numerous scars—including a deformed little finger—but his left is totally unmarked. Whenever he has had cause to crash a fist through glass, concrete or someone else's face it has always been the right one. The left hand has remained protected.

Once, one of those black-veiled ladies suggested he use the period set aside for drawing to portray a scene that he knew well. It was a foolhardy idea that the simple virginal nun could never have anticipated. He drew a horse. That was innocent enough. The nuns knew that he hailed from Connemara. They struggled not to be so virtuous as to condemn outright the link he was demonstrating with his father's profession. After all, the parish priest had been known to provide 'the Captain' with a certain amount of custom from time to time. But this lady of virtue was walking into a trap of her own digging. She was not satisfied with Peter's horse. 'Make it more interesting,' she instructed. 'Let him be doing something. Show something more.'

He did—and the nun first blushed and then brought down the ruler even more firmly on the boy's right hand. To the rear of the hapless animal Peter had added a huge penis—from which was gushing a torrent of urine. It was the sort of shock treatment he would later bring to his theatrical performances and the result now was no less effective.

Peter considered that the nuns, and all they stood for, were so unnatural. 'Their whole denial of womanhood,' he told the *New York Times* in 1972, 'the black dresses, the shaving of the hair, was so horrible, so terrifying. Of course, that's all been stopped. They're sipping gin and tonic in the Dublin pubs now. A couple of them flashed their pretty ankles at me just the other day.'

The nuns who were his teachers did not go into the pubs or flash pretty ankles. They would have been none too pleased to know that Peter belonged to a group he has since called MM, the Mutual Masturbation Society. 'It was considered a healthy alternative to ordinary sex,' he explains. It was to be the nearest thing to a homosexual experience in his life.

But Peter's relationship with the Church was not totally strained. For a long time, he was an altar boy for the priest who was eventually to become the Catholic primate of England, Cardinal Heenan. Like many a future actor, the theatricality of the role was the feature of the ritual that appealed most. But he did wonder about what he saw as the hypocrisy of it all.

At the age of eleven he moved to another school in Leeds into the hands of Jesuit priests. One of them—in a nice switch from more conventional schoolboy stories—he spotted smoking during prayers. He could see a wisp of blue smoke rising from beneath his cassock. Since Peter was never the kind to keep back from stating what was on his mind, he approached the hapless cleric, 'Is that all right, Sir?' he asked him. 'Isn't it a sin?'

The priest decided it was more sensible not to try to deny the offence. 'You're not as clever as I was when I was your age,' he replied. 'When the Bishop caught me doing this, I said to him, "Is it all right if I pray when I'm smoking?" '

Peter liked that.

It was a tough neighbourhood where fighting seemed as natural as the smoke seeping into the blackening brickwork.

14

There were Jews, Italians and a few Asians—all elbowing each other for room just as their houses seemed to be stretching and begging for air. What was more, each community divided itself into a gang that sought 'justice' on the streets.

The O'Tooles moved house almost as frequently as his father escaped from racetracks. At one time they lived outside Coventry. It was not a good idea. The industrial city was devasted by German bombers—the O'Toole house included. Peter recalls walking with his sister after the raid and seeing a dead woman and her child lying in the road. And then they saw a huge giraffe on its side surrounded by salt and pepper pots. They had been blown out of the nearby science museum which had been wrecked in the raid. The giraffe, needless to say, had been stuffed, and the salt and pepper pots came from the museum restaurant. Being bombed was to have a lasting impression on Peter. It gave him a sense of cameradery with every other victim of the war. He felt brave, and he was to say: 'You play this mad, demented, passive role. I tell you, if you haven't been bombed, you haven't lived. Perhaps if more people had been bombed, they might be less generous in their supply of bombs.'

He was a very committed Catholic in those days, as happens with so many children of that age. In fact he says himself that he suffered a severe attack of 'handmaidens' knee' from all his time in church. After the bombing he lived with a priest, Father Leo Walsh, who had just been ordained. Together, they used to rise at six and celebrate Mass. When he acted as Father Walsh's own altar boy, he felt that the priest was the star of a show and he was the understudy.

At the age of fifteen he decided he had stopped believing and told Father Walsh he was giving up religion. Since that time he says he has been a 'retired Christian'. In a celebrated *Playboy* interview with Kenneth Tynan he described his attitude to religion.

'I believe, as John Le Carré says in one of his books, that the Number 11 bus goes to Hammersmith and that Santa Claus isn't driving it. And I believe in Ghandi's marvellous, ironic, remark that God has no right to appear to mankind except in the shape of bread. What a lovely flip of the Catholic coin! But it took me a long time to believe in transubstantiation. If you're a Catholic, you aren't a sinner as long as you can drop in at what they call the "short twelve"—12 o'clock Mass. It's there for actors, writers, painters and other drunks, and it's short because the priest needs a drink like everybody else. All they do is elevate the Host, and if you witness the transubstantiation—the changing of the bread into Christ's body and the wine into his blood—you're home and dry.'

But he was neither home in the church, nor dry in his leisure pursuits as an adolescent when he was back in Leeds. He had already discovered that he liked a drink or two, although he kept it under control. The memory of the people he knew in those days has remained with him ever since. It might be a girl he knew when he was six years old, or boys with whom he teased the nuns and who nicknamed him—somewhat embarrassingly—Bubbles after his mop of unruly, blond hair.

It was at school that he discovered Shakespeare for the first time and found a talent for writing himself. At fifteen, he was penning verses like this:

> 'I don't crave security.
> I want to hazard my soul to opportunity.'

As if to help him with his work, he always carried a volume of Shakespeare in his back pocket. It was a practice that was to last.

He walked off with all the English composition prizes. One of his pieces, he remembers, was about a village idiot he had known, named Obadiah—a man who was teased unmercifully when he went into the pub and was served a noxious mixture ranging from *crème de menthe* to aftershave lotion. When the man was thrown out he was delightedly happy. For the first time in his life he had been accepted as part of a group. Peter called his essay, 'A Sound of

16

Revelry'. It would be a sound he would himself hear many times in the future.

When he left school, it was to take a job in a local warehouse, wrapping parcels. It taught him two things, both of which he has never forgotten—that he had to make his living in a different way from that chosen by most of his contemporaries, and how to tie string and then break it without needing to use a pair of scissors.

When he got fed up with the job that seemed to offer no opportunity at all, he left the warehouse determined to embark on a new career—as a journalist.

Two

PETER SEAMUS O'TOOLE took a job as a copyboy at the offices of the *Yorkshire Evening News* not just to get away from the rut of the warehouse, but because it would give him the perfect chance to write. There was also another reason; one that he put into the second part of the verse he wrote before changing jobs:

> '*I will not be a common man because it is my*
> *right to be an uncommon man.*
> *I will stir the smooth sands of monotony.*'

He was there for four years. From being a copyboy, he went to the paper's darkroom, where he became a photographer's assistant. He was also allowed to try his hand at writing the odd news story—until the news editor told him that he didn't think he would ever make a good journalist. It wasn't completely heartbreaking news.

Recently, Peter has said that at seventeen, he was terribly unsure exactly what he wanted to do. If he was not totally sure what was going to happen, he was completely certain what would not come to pass. He was thinking as deeply about his potential—or lack of potential—in newspapers as he had previously thought about the Church, or about following in his father's footsteps and becoming a bookie. And he had already decided that he would get out at the first opportunity. The reason was simple: this 'uncommon man' had come to the conclusion that the people who recorded the lives

of famous men and women rarely become famous themselves. There were altogether too few Dr Johnsons to a
seemingly never-ending supply of Boswells. He wanted
people to write about him, not the other way around.

He had already found a taste for things that were going to
set him apart. Certainly, these were not restricted to the
thirst he had already discovered for some of the finer things in
life, like girls and booze—and not necessarily in that order.

He had already developed a political antenna, which told
him, like a number of other young people, that the workers
were being exploited by the employing classes. The only
salvation on offer came via the Communist Party. 'They did a
lot for me when I was young,' he has said. But then he wasn't
thinking solely of their political contribution. 'They had the
best amateur repertory theatre in Leeds,' he explained. And
the theatre was taking on ever new and important dimensions
in his life. Standing on the stage in local halls produced sparks
in his mind that soon turned into blazing fires.

He wanted—he needed—to see the theatre that
counted—in London. So he and a friend, a painter from
Leeds called Patrick Oliver, decided to try their luck hitch-
ing. They hitch-hiked via Stratford-on-Avon, where they
bought the cheapest tickets to see Michael Redgrave in *King
Lear*. It was perhaps the most valuable investment Peter
O'Toole ever made. He now knew for certain what he
wanted to do with his life. His choice of sleeping accommodation that night was not, however, quite so satisfactory.

In the almost drunken stupor brought on by the heady
experience of Redgrave's Lear, they found their way to an
empty field and selected a haystack. His friend fell asleep
immediately. Peter was too occupied with other thoughts to
go off quite so easily. Idly, he started digging with his bare
hands into the interior of the stack. His friend, he discovered,
was sleeping quite blissfully on a dungheap. Peter neither
forgot the experience, nor the location of the 'bed'!

He knew it would be quite easy for his life to turn into
something almost as unpleasant—unless he did something

19

very concrete. He had no doubt that he was going to be an actor. He knew, too, that he was going to be a very successful one. All that had to be worked out was precisely how that state of affairs would come about. It wasn't, however, the easiest time to ponder the point. Young men of eighteen were required to do National Service, a surrender of two years to King and country in the army, navy or air force. The idea made him feel less than ecstatic, especially now that he knew where his future lay, but there was little alternative short of emigrating permanently to Ireland, going down the mines or agreeing to spend three or four years in the even less salubrious surroundings of Leeds Prison. He contemplated registering as a conscientious objector, but the conscientious objections he had been making to attending Mass since the age of fifteen acted heavily against such a proposal.

Having weighed up the possibilities before him, Peter decided he would join the navy. The days of the press gangs were long over, but life in the Senior Service was fairly tough. It was not quite as simple as merely making a choice and donning a pair of bell-bottoms. In fact it was immensely difficult to persuade the Royal Navy to take in any young man as a national serviceman. For one thing, they insisted on both parents being British born, and for the chief petty officer in the recruiting office there was no certainty that Ireland counted—even if it had been part of the British Empire when Patrick Joseph O'Toole was born.

That was when Peter did his first piece of serious acting. 'But I have to tell you,' he said, fixing the bemused man in blue with those steely eyes of his, 'I come from a long line of seafaring men. My father is the famous Captain O'Toole who sailed the Atlantic before I was born.'

It would only have confused the issue, he has since said, to explain that the 'Captain' was a bookmaker.

Against most of the odds, he was accepted. He was due to report to Portsmouth on the day he had his first audition at the Nottingham Playhouse. He decided he could do both—although how much use he would be to the theatre

20

with two years' National Service ahead defies the imagination. He turned up for the audition readily armed with a speech or two from *Macbeth*. Faced with a vast, empty stage, a spotlight all but blinding him and a none too sympathetic producer sitting in the stalls, he coughed nervously—and couldn't remember a line he was supposed to recite.

'All right, Mr O'Rourke,' said the producer—getting the name wrong seemed to put the situation into perfect if soul-destroying perspective. 'Let's not waste any more of each other's time, shall we?'

It would not be the only time that the supposedly unluckiest play in the English language would cause Peter O'Toole a problem or two. For the moment, however, no problem would be greater than his struggles with the navy.

Before his true value to His Majesty had been assessed during that misguided period in 1950, someone suggested that he might make officer material. He was tall and good-looking enough to be featured on a recruiting poster. He had already begun to train his voice to have an upper-class accent—although there would always be highly recognisable ingredients of Yorkshire in his speech. He also had a tendency to lisp and, very occasionally, stammer.

He was 'invited' to take a test—none of it too taxing; just twenty questions mainly to establish his potential for using initiative. If he passed this stage, he would go on to an officer training school.

'How,' he was asked, 'would you get a heavy barrel over a wall thirty foot high if you only had two lengths of rope, each ten foot long? 'Easy,' said Peter, without thinking too long, 'I would say to the Chief petty officer, "Chief petty officer, get that barrel over that wall".'

The answer was no more audacious than the idea of him submitting himself for the exam in the first place.

He was recommended for service with submarines and was trained as a signalman. But more than that, he was training himself to get out of the navy. The idea of Peter Seamus O'Toole wearing bell-bottoms and accepting the authority of other people for whom life began and ended in the sea, struck him as faintly ridiculous.

Accordingly, he rebelled whenever the opportunity arose. Now, everyone knows that the area beneath one's feet on board a ship—which he insisted on calling a boat—is the deck. Peter always said it was the floor. The glass through which the sea outside could be clearly seen was, of course, shaped in the form of portholes. He never described them as anything but windows. He managed to send a visiting senior officer into fits of apoplexy by referring to a ship's funnel as 'that chimney'.

His time seemed to be divided between playing in the ship's band, and being seasick. He had found out how to bang a bass drum in time, 'It was so easy,' he told actor Roy Kinnear a few years later. 'All you had to do was be able to go "boom" at the right moment.' As for being seasick, this was perhaps the most serious offence of all. 'I polluted the waters of the seven seas with the contents of my stomach,' he has said referring to those times, sailing the Baltic Sea and the North Atlantic.

When he was on duty on deck, he would look out to sea, reciting Shakespeare. Sometimes, he talked to the seagulls. All of which made him seem strange indeed to most of the people on board.

He continued to search for ways of parting from the Lords of the Admiralty. But despite his lack of enthusiasm and inability to conform, they seemed remarkably loath to let him go. A friend had told him that a sure-fire way of earning his release ticket was to drink great quantities of alcohol combined with generous supplies of aspirin. It would, he was told, give him an unhealthy-looking grey pallor. Thus, in the course of a single night, he consumed eighteen bottles of wine together with sufficient tablets to send most men into a coma. The next day he was pretty groggy. His face, however, was no more pallid than was usual when he was feeling seasick.

The following evening he was in his hammock, darning socks and telling anyone who would listen how little he enjoyed being in a submarine: 'For Christ's sake, I get claustrophobia in a lift!' He was even heard to tell an officer, 'This is such a bloody waste of time.' It became particularly apparent when he was required to do marching. Quite genuinely he didn't know his left foot from his right.

The navy's patience was wearing out. One bitterly cold day he was arrested for insubordination and for stealing an extra ration of coal, and was thrown in the brig.

His charm with women was to get him into trouble, too. Peter was less than happy with the requirement that he learn to decode messages. For one thing, he found it very hard to understand. For another, it seemed such a dreadful waste of time. What on earth—or even on sea—would he do with naval codes when he was the principal actor at Stratford-on-Avon? If *Hamlet* had been written in Morse then he would have been happy to learn it. But the movement of ships? My dear chap . . .

Fortunately, he had got to know a pretty little officer in the Wrens who was immediately won over by this exceedingly unable seaman.

He was known as a 'brown-card' rating—which meant he was able to get ashore fairly frequently. Conveniently, the young lady was responsible for sending out the ships' weather forecasts. Between them, they hit on the idea of Peter phoning her when he got on dry land—during which time she would supply him with all the information he required without the bother of having to spend anything up to two hours deciphering the code.

The ploy was discovered—navy telephones are never the most private of instruments—and the officer was dismissed. Peter was once more thrown into the brig.

It was but another minor misdemeanour in his naval career. There were so many others that he cannot recall them all at a single sitting. But a visit to Sweden—the first made by the fleet since 1939—gave his commanding officer as many reasons to keep him away from civilisation as anything else.

The admiral was due to be welcomed on the jetty by

Sweden's King Gustav VI Adolf. Everything was planned in the usual navy way—or rather what had been the usual navy way prior to O'Toole's arrival—except that no one had bargained for a sudden blanket of fog cutting off His Britannic Majesty's ships from His Swedish Majesty's harbour.

Peter was instructed to accompany a junior officer on a hazardous trip ashore, and then signal back by walkie-talkie when contact had been made with the Swedes. Their barge was totally alone in the dense, grey mist when Peter decided to lean over the side to see if he could see more than he could hear through the instrument's earpiece. It was not a clever thing to do. The walkie-talkie had only been strapped over one shoulder—instead of two as naval regulations required—and as its custodian leaned over the side, it slipped down over his arm into the murky, deep and invisible Swedish waters.

It was the brig again for that.

For reasons that seem to defy either logic or explanation, nothing in his behaviour indicated to the Royal Navy on this visit that his recreational activities ought to be curbed. When it was deemed sensible to field a rugby team to play the Swedish locals, Peter was instructed to take part.

It turned out not to be a wise move, and once again a woman was involved in the result. She turned out to be not just blonde, pretty and have a curvy figure, but she was also a nurse, whose attentions he would need after the rugby game.

She was not, however, all that useful before the game started. Like a number of females for whom life consists of more than just the events on a sports field, she found it difficult to work out the differences between rugby and soccer. When Peter asked her to drive him to the ground—after a leave which he should not have taken—she got lost. Together, they visited all the soccer stadia in Stockholm, none of which had ever seen a rugby ball. They arrived just two minutes before the opening whistle was blown.

O'Toole got to the ground only to be told that the team had been changed. Someone else was in his usual position and he would have to get his head down and join the scrum, not a role that he relished. The forwards in the scrum are usually as broad as he was tall. They either attack or suffer the inevitable consequences. This was an occasion when Peter decided that playing the rules of the game could only serve to his disadvantage.

He came out of the scrum feeling rather like a piece of putty, and bearing a distinct resemblance to one, too. He was transferred to the role of full-back, a normally quiet, defensive position where the object of the exercise is to stay where you are and make sure no one from the opposite side usurps your position.

Peter got as tired of that as he did of the rules imposed by the navy. After kicking his heels for too long in that passive position, he grabbed the ball and ran with it over the whole length of the pitch. He then scored. It increased the British tally but it wasn't really cricket any more than it was rugby, and there were apologetic frowns from the team captain and coach directed at the other side. 'They said it was pure selfishness,' he has recalled.

If it was, it wasn't the kind of behaviour any self-respecting Scandinavian athlete—who in this case happened to be a policeman—was going to allow. The man in question decided to take the first possible opportunity to let the Englishman know that he and national honour felt mortally offended.

Seeing the amused O'Toole in close proximity, the blond giant fixed him with a stare that wouldn't have seemed any more fierce had a pair of horns been attached to his head. With the full weight of his body—to say nothing of his massive boot—the Swede kicked Peter in the chin. It had an instant effect. Peter bit his tongue and practically severed it in the process.

He was rushed to the nearest hospital where the damage was repaired. Still feeling as though a rugby ball was clamped between his teeth, he was released in time to rejoin the fleet before it sailed down the North Sea for home. He was directed to the nearest railway station and helped aboard the train for Stockholm. The patient was, however, rather more anxious to see his nurse (and not exactly for medical reasons) than he was to get back to the ship.

Unfortunately, as luck would have it, he was on the wrong train going in the wrong direction. Not only could he not speak the language to enable him to extricate himself from the situation, but he couldn't speak English either. A series of groans and grunts got him on the right train and on the right line for the capital. The nurse was still waiting for him at the station and prepared, with no alternative in view other than seeing him incarcerated in a Royal Navy cell, to drive him to the quayside.

When they did get there, it was clear that the sirens had sounded, the captain had been piped aboard, and all hands were on deck—except Peter's. The fleet had sailed and there was no way of getting him aboard any of the vessels now steaming towards the horizon. There was, however, one not so obvious solution.

It was the nurse who spotted an amusement park boat, fully bedecked in bunting, at the quayside. While the stupefied O'Toole stood there, literally dumbstruck, she hired the boat, virtually threw Peter on it and watched it move out to sea, flags and balloons trailing in the water as they chugged towards one of His Majesty's principal arms of defence. It had been the first use of a 'little boat' for naval operations since Dunkirk. Only this time, no one could be sure that the Admiralty were quite so pleased.

Peter recovered from both the ordeal and the operation on his tongue. The latter had an effect he could not have anticipated the day he was wheeled into surgery in the Swedish hospital. Both his stammer and most of his lisp vanished. So it seems had much of the navy's enthusiasm to keep him in their midst. Now every time he was arrested, and every time he found ways of making himself ill, the file on seaman Peter Seamus O'Toole was looked at more and more closely.

Finally, eighteen months after he was first recruited at Portsmouth, he went before a naval board and was judged to be temperamentally unsuited to the life of a sailor. He was discharged.

For reasons that will never be totally clear, he walked out of the Portsmouth barracks where he signed the papers which meant that he could never be called to serve his country again—even in the event of a national emergency—with a brown paper package containing his entire sailor's uniform: bell-bottoms, wide collar, black neck ribbon (it was meant to be a sign of mourning for Nelson, not for the departure of Peter O'Toole). He caught the train to London and as he left Waterloo station he meandered slowly towards Chelsea Bridge.

It was from there, and with no due ceremony, he threw the parcel into the water. He watched, fascinated, as the package disappeared under the water. Even more magnetic was the sight of his white sailor's cap at first floating and then very, very slowly, sinking, an appropriate gesture it seemed, like a ship going down with its ensign flying. What he remembers most about that moment was seeing the whiteness of the cap disappear beneath the murky grey of the water. Ever since then he has had a profound dislike of anything white. But it was the happiest burial at sea a sailor was ever called upon to witness.

Now, he had only one ambition in mind, or at least temporary ambition. To study drama.

Three

THE ROYAL ACADEMY of Dramatic Art is not only just a stones's throw from London's West End, it is also in the heart of Bloomsbury, nestled between the capital's university and, numerous other centres of learning in Gower Street—the home of University College, its world-famous hospital, and its various medical schools.

It is an appropriate location for what is internationally regarded as one of the great drama schools. Its reputation can be gauged by the fact that it is one of the few institutions instantly identified by its initials alone. Not all the great actors and actresses of the world learned their craft at RADA and not all the people who study there become great, but enough of them do to make gaining a place there one of the great dreams of a young man or woman with ambition to go on the stage.

It is so important that some of those ambitious youngsters go there just to stand around and imbibe the atmosphere, in much the same way as a budding journalist would soak in the ink-scented noise and bustle of London's Fleet Street. The buildings are nothing in themselves, but what they represent is everything.

Peter O'Toole knew that RADA was where he wanted to be. So he went. And as he walked through the main lobby of the building, the tall figure was stopped by a man trained by long experience to spot a potential actor almost by instinct.

'What do you want?' he was asked. 'I want to come here,' he replied. 'Well, you can have an audition,' said the man, who happened to be Sir Kenneth Barnes, the academy principal.

Peter had his audition. He recited pieces from Shakespeare, answered a few questions in writing, and was rewarded with a scholarship. All his fees would be paid and there was to be a grant, too. It could have been seen as an answer to his prayers. To Peter it was merely the first concrete step on the way to that success he knew would be his.

Twelve months earlier, Sir Kenneth Barnes had granted a place to a slightly older actor named Frank Finlay, and when Peter walked in for his first lesson in voice production, he found among the new boys and girls hopefuls named Richard Harris, Alan Bates, Albert Finney, Bryan Pringle, Roy Kinnear, Ronald Fraser and Rosemary Leach. It was apparent that Sir Kenneth had spotted some considerable talent over the last year or two.

Most of these students were from the north of England—'a fact that Sir Kenneth couldn't cope with at all,' another of their number, actress Shirley Dixon, told me. 'We were all a north country bunch—with Peter combining his northern upbringing with that peculiar Irish charm.' To the few southerners in their year, they seemed a particular threat, a sort of Yorkshire mafia.

It was probably the most potentially star-encrusted student body even RADA had ever had in one session, and Peter appreciated the value of being in that set right from the beginning. 'My whole life changed,' he has said. It is also fair to say that his fellow students appreciated being with him from the moment he recited his first line on the stage, the first real stage he had ever worked on. It was in a play called *The Appleyards,* and in his walk-on role all he had to say was 'It's a nice band.' That could also have referred to the other people at RADA with him. They certainly regarded having Peter with them as a plus factor.

'I knew then that he was exceptional,' Roy Kinnear told me. 'His talent was obvious for all to see,' says Frank Finlay. But he adds, 'One is often coloured by things that happen subsequently and I have to say that Peter at the time was not included in any list of those one thought was great.' He was,

29

however, to change that assessment as the years at RADA went on.

Frank and Peter fenced together regularly, but their first meeting on stage was in the still-celebrated performance of Dylan Thomas's *Under Milk Wood*. 'I remember Peter came on with a bucket. All he said was one line—but he brought the house down.'

That evening has to be remembered as the first public performance of the play. Peter's part as No Good Boyo is still talked about by those who were in the cast—practically the whole of that RADA year. By all accounts it was certainly a portrait not to be forgotten.

To some, Peter's acting talent became obvious in his earliest weeks there. Like every other student, he was expected to prepare plays and learn about their authors. While most of them, however, were content just to read the plays and the usual biographical notes, Peter would come to classes with an armful of books, telling not just the life of the playwright, but the period in which he lived, the background to the first production of the work and the style and critical response to drama in that particular era. There were, nevertheless, occasions when he was singularly unprepared.

Like everyone else at RADA, Peter had to be willing for his work to be dissected like one of the bodies on slabs in the medical schools a hundred or so yards away. It wasn't long before he felt he was spreading his wings widely enough and working sufficiently hard at the academy to demand parts. 'There's no such thing,' said the instructor, 'as small parts. Only small actors.' It was advice that was difficult to forget and Peter has himself referred to it time after time. It resulted in him making a decision for himself—he wanted the smallest parts thereafter, just so that he could prove both to the tutor and his fellow students exactly what he could do with them.

But he got the big roles, too. Ernest Milton directed his Malvolio in the academy production of *Twelfth Night*. At the dress rehearsal an actor playing a smaller part was late. He explained that Peter had asked him to get a stick that he needed to complete his Malvolio ensemble. 'I will not have anyone fetching things for Peter O'Toole,' said the director, which served to bring Peter down a peg or two.

He wasn't the most obedient or subservient of RADA students and there were times when he plainly showed a contempt for the instructors and their direction. 'My God,' one fellow student heard him say more than once. 'What the hell does he know? If he were any good he wouldn't be teaching here, would he?' It was not an entirely fair judgment, for not only were a number of the RADA directors highly competent, but some were semi-retired professionals who in their day had had international reputations. Others were practising directors who just liked to teach.

Roy Kinnear remembers: 'He'd never take direction. He'd just tell the director a thing or two and leave. That's the confidence of youth. Only when you get older do you start to care and worry. Peter would tell the director how he was going to do a scene and then do it.'

His tussles with one member of the Academy's staff have gone down into the establishment's folklore.

Lionel Marsden was the lecturer in voice production. All the students were expected to prepare a speech for his lesson and Marsden would then give him his assessment of the performance. On this occasion, Peter failed to come with anything in hand.

'That's all right,' said Marsden. 'Read something out of here'—and handed him a book.

The experience was rather like sitting in on a great musician's masterclass, except that the pupil was somewhat less willing to take part in the show. Peter started to read.

'No, no,' said Marsden, 'do it again.'

Once more Peter started to read. He had gone through just a couple of lines when Marsden interrupted again. 'No,' he said. 'No, no, no.'

The student looked at the master, picked up the book and threw it at him. Peter O'Toole made his exit and didn't appear at the class for more than a week. Then he apologised.

What struck Roy Kinnear about the Peter O'Toole he knew at that time was his 'fantastic, boundless energy'. He had, Kinnear told me, 'an amazing stamina, a great capacity for enjoying life. There was an excitement about his talent. When you're young, you can get away with energy as a substitute for talent, but he had both. There was a magic there that we knew was absolutely exceptional.' And not just in his dramatic work. His whole appearance indicated his brilliance. 'He had a magnificent nose.' That was what made the big impression in those days and seemed to strike almost everyone who came across him.

'Strike!' says Kinnear, only partly joking. 'You had to duck! A great crinkled thing, but not ugly.' It wasn't broken or misshapen, but a ski-jump nose that many people remember as adding a great deal to his physical attraction.

In addition to actual experience practising his craft, and the lessons in voice production, there were lectures on Shakespeare and the other great dramatists, discussions on acting technique, as well as instruction in fencing and ballet.

'It was also a great time for pulling in the birds,' Peter has since said.

Shirley Dixon told me that the birds were quite anxious to pull him in, too. 'He was bold and sure—the tremendous contrast between the strength one knew was there and his gentleness. He was physically tremendously attractive—and always laughing.'

Peter actually lost a pound in a bet concerning Miss Dixon, whom he had let it be known among the company he fancied more than somewhat, while they were working together in *Under Milk Wood,* in which she played Polly Garter. She was not known for the ease with which she accepted dates from male students, a fact that Peter had refused to allow to disturb him.

Another young hopeful bet O'Toole ten shillings that she wouldn't sleep with him and another ten that she wouldn't even go out with him. Peter had to borrow a pound's worth of drinking money to honour the bet.

'He came up to me with that wonderful line about how good I was in the play and asked me for supper. Well, my heart stood still. I was so frightened, I said no. I didn't think I could cope with someone quite so attractive. There was always a great deal of talk about his exploits with the ladies. Now I think to myself, What a fool! How could I be so stupid! What a shame!'

It was plainly a great time for socialising. There was a constant round of one party after another. At one of these, Roy Kinnear told me, Peter drank a whole bottle of Scotch in a single swig—as though downing that staple of most drinking competitions, a yard of ale.

'Cheers,' said Peter, and the fight was on.

'He came up for air a couple of times,' said Roy, 'but apart from that, it went down in one go.'

At one party orchestrated by Peter on a houseboat where he then lived at Brentford, the entire crowd fell into the Thames when the boat flooded. 'We all took turns at the pumps, coming up all over the place like moles,' said Frank Finlay. The celebrations ended at the Lyons Corner House restaurant in the Strand.

Not that he moved in one particular set all the time. Finlay told me that he was sure Peter 'never had any particular mates or girlfriends. But he had the facility of knowing where all the parties were being held. We also found the pubs where beer was a ha'penny cheaper than in most other places.' And not just the beer. Together, they discovered the joys of Merrydown cider—without realising at first just how potent the stuff is.

It was also a chance to get some practice in the various branches of acting, to say nothing of earning a few meagre pounds to supplement the grants. Announcements would appear on the academy notice boards offering anything from auditions to tiny jobs in low budget films, because for some a place at RADA was sufficient to earn an Equity card.

There was no union at the time for stuntmen, and they were frequently in demand—especially those who didn't mind getting into knife fights, or who could fence or ride. Peter was willing and able to do all those things and in numerous now-forgotten period movies made between 1952 and 1955, the back of an actor riding off in the sunset could well be that of a young, inexperienced and impecunious Peter O'Toole.

'Sometimes,' he told writer Tim Satchell, 'you'd get hurt. You'd go into the gents and want to die. But somehow, you survived.' He likes to quote an old rhyme which he mangles delightedly:

> *'There was a young man called Ned*
> *Who fell down the stairs on his head*
> *When they asked why he did it,*
> *He said I do it for a living.'*

But he paid the price of that living. 'I seem to remember,' says Shirley Dixon, 'that he would constantly appear for a class with something or other in plaster. He was always breaking one part of his anatomy or another.'

Somehow he found it easier than ballet. Malcolm Rogers who was another member of that RADA year told me: 'It was difficult at the age of twenty-plus to don ballet shoes for the first time and he didn't exactly take his ballet very seriously.' In fact, his greatest attribute during this time was being able to watch out for the ballet mistress to turn her back so that he could kick the dancer in front of him.

That teacher was unlikely to have been invited to one of the parties Peter held at the various addresses at which he was living. He has said that he stayed in more than twenty-five different rooms during his three years at RADA, once sharing one of those rooms with six other people and living on spaghetti and tomato sauce.

He used to dress, says one writer remembering those days, 'as if he were late for an appointment with a means test'.

And as Roy Kinnear remembers, the favourite question

from his fellow students each morning was: 'Hello, Peter, which hedge did you sleep under last night?'

He always seemed to wear the same thing, a pair of corduroy trousers which got more and more shabby as the term wore on and a jersey which might have benefited from a darning needle.

What he could put on—and with amazing style and panache—were the inner clothes of the characters he played. When they performed *The Linden Tree* at RADA, Peter *became* an older man. It wasn't a case of painting lines on his face and tinting his hair with grey—every actor does that and hopes he looks older as a result, which none of them do. When Peter did it, there was a sense that he knew what it was like to line up for an old-age pension on a Thursday.

When he got drunk, there were unpleasant meetings with policemen. More than once, he ended up in court. Sometimes, when the misdemeanours of others came before the attention of the magistrates, he had to appear as a witness. It was one of these occasions that he appeared in court plainly not wearing any socks.

'Don't you have any socks?' asked a policeman before going into the courtroom.

'Of course, I have,' he said.

'Well, where are they?' asked the policeman.

'They're here,' said O'Toole producing a somewhat mangey pair of green hose from his pocket. He wears green socks to this day—with sports trousers or a dinner suit—but they are usually in better condition than those he produced for the benefit of the law that day.

Of course, Peter didn't care. Neither did he worry much about his sense of being a 'professional'. During academy vacations he and Malcolm Rogers, who also hailed from Leeds, used to take part in the productions of the city's leading amateur group, the Civic Theatre. One of his best roles with the company was in *A Month In The Country*. He was in the middle of a production there when their first

RADA reports came through the post. Rogers scored seventy-seven percent, Peter seventy-eight.

To help make very frayed ends meet, Peter took jobs during the holidays. He sold curtains at Schofield's store in Leeds and delivered Christmas cards and parcels for the Post Office.

There were other people at RADA for whom Peter had an instinctive respect. He never forgot the advice of one of his tutors, Hugh Miller, who told him, 'Never play checkers with your career.' He says he has always remembered that advice, but fails to admit that he hasn't always taken it to heart—which he quite plainly has not.

It is true to say that he worried a number of the directors and others who were teaching him at the academy, people who recognised his talent but were concerned about his personality. As Roy Kinnear told me: 'People whom you know are going to be stars are likely to be dangerous—not physically dangerous, but under the aura of it all, there is plainly something bubbling.

'In those days, they just expected you to be very nice. I think at one time, we did nothing but come in and out of French windows, wearing black bow ties!'

And, he remembers, Peter wasn't always very good. 'I've seen him be absolutely terrible, dreadfully wrong—so bad that it's marvellous. You know, it takes a genius to be as bad as that sometimes. Ordinary actors can't be that bad.'

Sir Kenneth Barnes was the main arbiter of a student's success in those days. He would sit in a little box at the back of the theatre where they performed, his dog at his side. As Royal Kinnear says: 'If his dog liked it, you were all right.' The next day, all the cast would assemble in Sir Kenneth's little room, notebooks to hand, and absorb his critiques.

Peter's brushes with authority certainly did not mean that he was not influenced by older actors. There were many whom he greatly admired. He was sitting on a London underground train once, reading a script and with the faraway look on his face of one trying hard to remember something important. He felt a tap on the shoulder. 'Not in public,' said his fellow passenger. 'Never in public.' It was the eminent actor Wilfrid Lawson, who wanted to know more about the young man sitting next to him. By the time their journey had come to an end, they had arranged to meet again. Lawson became a close friend and their times together turned into impromptu acting lessons.

'He also taught me how to drink,' Peter told the London *Sunday Express*. Lawson had become 'my guide, actor and friend. He's an actor to be cherished.'

So, of course, were many of his fellow students, and not just those who have become celebrated household names as he has himself. There was something very special about that generation. As he once put it to the *New York Times:* 'We weren't reckoned for much at the time. We were all considered dotty. Even then, we were all dissenters. It was the time of Korea and we wanted to know what it was all about, this war to keep back the hordes of reddish yellows, yellow reds or whatever.

'You see, we all shared the common experience of being war babies, of being bombed, of being evacuated, of facing compulsory service.'

Indeed, Peter's National Service was the subject of much of his conversation at the time, how he won his war with the navy. He offered little pieces of advice to students who were going to have to break up their time at the academy by doing their duty.

The graduation ceremony at RADA is, in effect, the 'last show', the final performance of a play in which most of the year's cast take part, in a large London theatre before a hopefully crowded audience—to say nothing of an assembly of Fleet Street critics, searching for new talent and the possibility of being able to say, a few years hence, that they had been the first to point out the callow youth who was now an established star. Alas, no critic can now say that he spotted Peter O'Toole that far back. Or if he did, he wasn't able to write about it.

It was to be Pirandello's *Right You Are If You Think So* or *The Rules of The Game*. As always, Peter went into the task as though he were studying for his BA degree course, or at least 'A' levels. Day after day he spent at the British Museum—'a rehearsal of discovery' says Frank Finlay.

The RADA class of 1955 had to manage without critical acclaim of any kind. Their show was performed in the midst of the first national newspaper strike for nearly thirty years. But there were a number of members of the cast who thought that Peter would get the accolade of the academy, the Bancroft Gold Medal. By all accounts, his appearance that night was brilliant.

It was, however, an appearance he almost missed. He had been with his family in Leeds up to the day of the show and decided to travel down to London by road. A friend had offered him a lift in his car and when you are a student you take advantage of every opportunity to avoid paying a train fare. The fare would have been a better investment.

They were speeding down the A1 when their car crashed into a ten-ton lorry. The friend was seriously injured and, as it turned out, crippled for life. Peter himself was kept in hospital for five hours with leg injuries, but he knew he had to get back to London. In great pain, he stole back his clothes and crept out of the hospital. Back in London, he found a doctor to bandage the leg and give him a painkiller. He was on stage on time.

After the show, the entire company moved off to the little theatre where Sir Kenneth Barnes gave his assessment of their work. Finally, he said, 'the winner of the Bancroft Gold Medal is . . .' It was not his usual practice, but this time he paused. '. . . is Bryan . . .' A huge cheer went up and a number of the cast were banging Brian Bedford on the back in congratulation, 'is Bryan Pringle'. An outstanding actor of today had had his first recognition. Peter O'Toole, who had himself felt that his own part didn't lend itself to an award-winning performance, was in their midst offering his own good wishes. He would have to wait for a prize of his own. It wouldn't be long.

Four

BRISTOL, SITUATED AT the estuary of the River Severn, is one of Britain's loveliest cities—a port and an industrial centre in the heart of the west country. Its university—formed from a collection of architect-designed buildings—and the nearby boys' public school of Clifton, add to a cultural tradition that long ago set Bristol apart from other cities. And because of that cultural tradition, life for many in Bristol seems to revolve around the theatre. Before the age of the motorway, which has taken the city a mere two and a half hours away from the capital, it was a long, arduous journey to London, so it was natural that it should seek its own stage. You could, therefore, see anything from a big, brash American musical at the Hippodrome to *As You Like It* at the Theatre Royal.

The Royal was about 190 years old in the mid-fifties and for a great deal of that time had been the home of one of the most important repertory companies in the country. The Bristol Old Vic, then the 'daughter' organisation of London's famous classical theatre, was administered—if with a certain amount of autonomy—by London's Old Vic.

That was where Peter O'Toole set his sights when that last RADA show was finished. Bristol was holding auditions and he was going to offer himself for consideration. More than that, he was determined to dazzle them. Certainly he saw it as his big opportunity, and like all opportunities, it was there either to be grabbed or to be thrust aside. When Peter's ambition was first fired by the idea of working there, Bristol was not merely a nursery for the West End. In 1955, it was also a theatre that was sufficiently respected to be visited regularly by the Fleet Street critics. As such, it drew its audiences from far beyond the Severn estuary, and its players from all over the world.

Eric Porter was about to begin a new season there. So were Alan Dobie and Derek Godfrey. The company was filled and, like the cup in the psalms, showed a distinct inclination to run over. Nevertheless, John Moody, Bristol's artistic director, regarded it as something of a solemn obligation to hold auditions as though the theatre were starting from scratch, looking for a cast that ranged from the leading man and lady to the third spear-carrier on the right.

News of the auditions, to be conducted from the 'mother' theatre in London, not only appeared in *The Stage* and was spread from a hundred agents' offices but also featured on the notice boards of RADA and the other drama schools. It was to be one of the few times in Peter's career when he had an agent, and he was left in no doubt that the Bristol audition was something he ignored at his peril.

The sweater and corduroy trousers, now more threadbare than ever, took themselves off to the Waterloo Road theatre. Peter was full of the same confidence and certainty that had found expression at RADA. It wasn't a question of if he passed the audition, but when. He neither knew nor thought it relevant that the odds were stacked very high against all the other aspirants there that day.

Moody happened to be ill, but even that wouldn't excuse him from going through what he considered to be the correct motions for the annual ritual of auditions. If he couldn't attend them himself, then he had to install someone he could trust in his place. He asked his assistant Nat Brenner, then only five years into what would be an almost thirty-year career with the theatre (he was later to become general manager and head of the Bristol Old Vic School) to sit in the stalls and take notes.

There were a hundred people to see, young men and

women of considerable talent. However, none of them stood much of a chance of being offered a place at this most prestigious of provincial companies.

'It was a three-day haul,' Brenner told me. 'Not easy.' But it was at the end of those three days that a tall, spare youngster with piercing, blue eyes that within a decade would become an internationally recognised trademark, took his place on the stage and recited a speech or two from *Cyrano de Bergerac*. Peter O'Toole, blessed with a nose of his own which the character he was now playing would not have considered inadequate, made Brenner scribble furiously.

As Brenner recalls: 'I was very excited. He was absolutely riveting. A remarkable performance. I was absolutely smitten.' He was able, on the bare boards of the Old Vic stage, to convey all the agony that Cyrano felt, and make even a professional producer forget he was merely watching a performance. It was a rare moment and Brenner recognised it as such. If nothing else, it showed an intuitive ability to choose just the right material to make his listeners sit up and take notice.

He also chose an extract from *Berkeley Square,* in which he had to imagine he was talking to two women. He did it so brilliantly that unconsciously Brenner and the others sitting with him in the empty theatre found themselves looking for the women-like spectators at Wimbledon following a ball that was moving too fast for them to see.It was a scene recreated in a dozen Hollywood backstage musicals. A young unknown reciting a speech or singing a song for a hard-bitten producer who suddenly finds himself captivated. For once it was not a case of 'Don't call us, we'll call you'. Nat Brenner stopped Peter O'Toole in full flow.

'You're the first actor I've seen all day,' he said. 'Come forward.' And as O'Toole moved towards the footlights, Brenner told him he would do his best to get him a job with the company.

'It was,' he says now, 'a commitment.' Brenner recognised he had made a discovery of quite considerable proportions.

'Peter was there for discovering. If I hadn't found him, someone else would have.' He told me he spotted something else, too: 'I remember saying, even then, that I was facing a young man with a sense of self-destruction.' 'Do you drink?' he asked the spindly actor.

'A beer or two,' Peter replied.

'Well, don't let it go harder than that, for God's sake.'

Then he phoned John Moody. 'I've just seen a young man,' he said, 'who is quite remarkable.' It was, and he knew it, an understatement. 'We've got to make room for him.'

His big worry was that Moody would be 'sensible' and remind him that Bristol didn't need anyone for the next few months. Fortunately, ordinary good sense left him and he agreed to see Peter O'Toole. The company was about to open its season with Angus Wilson's new play, *The Mulberry Bush,* which had just been presented by the English Stage Company. The play was already cast. In fact, Moody was now making up his cast list for the third play of the season, *Ondine.* But Brenner begged him to use O'Toole.

Meanwhile, people from the London Old Vic were asked to come and see Brenner's new discovery. They did and were equally impressed. But he was Bristol's find and they wouldn't consider him for a London job if the junior theatre wanted him first. And Nat Brenner was determined that he should come to Bristol. He went even further—a gesture of enthusiasm not often shown by buyers in what is very clearly their own market—he suggested that Peter prepare himself with a speech from Shakespeare to further impress John Moody.

He did. He recited a few lines of Oberon's from *A Midsummer Night's Dream.* John Moody looked at his colleague and smiled.

'But what can we give him?' Moody asked.

'The cabdriver in *The Matchmaker?*' suggested Brenner. It was a part already sewn up. Anthony Tuckey was cast for the role, but he could be persuaded to give it up. It was a trial suggestion. If O'Toole came through the way they expected him to, there would be plenty of work for him to do both in *Ondine* and the play that was to follow, *Volpone*.

They were right. The cabdriver was only a cameo, but it contained the stuff of which great parts are created. Years later, Tuckey told Nat Brenner: 'I was very upset when I lost that part. But then when I saw Peter . . . marvellous!' Even with Eric Porter playing the lead role and the stage brimful of talented, competent performers, it was easy to see that Nat Brenner had made a discovery indeed. In fact it has been said that when Peter first appeared in the cabman's role he came on stage smelling of horses. He probably did.

It was not his only tiny role. In *Uncle Vanya,* his part was of a Georgian peasant who really had no more to say than 'Doctor Astrov, the horses have arrived,' and then he was supposed to lumber off. That was not the way Peter saw his role at all. He studied it as he would have the lead parts in the RADA productions. Georgia, he remembered, was where Stalin was born. Therefore the servant he played had to be like Stalin. The Russian dictator, he discovered, had a slight limp. So the servant would have one, too. He made himself up to look like Stalin—a man who would surely have a burning resentment for the Czarist aristocracy. This man would hate both his job and the man for whom he worked. He came on stage, with a sinister glare at his employer, and hissed: 'Dr Astrov, the horses have arrived!'

No one could say it was the way that Chekhov had planned it, but no one could deny either that it was a seriously thought-out ploy, a competent piece of theatre in less than a minute. It was certainly sufficiently competent for the actor to deserve the parts already earmarked for him in *Ondine* and *Volpone*.

Again, Brenner recalls now, watching him in those early performances, he found himself coming to precisely the same conclusions he came to at the Waterloo Road audition. And he was not the only one. Peter had not been at the Theatre Royal for long before his talent was being widely spoken about. John Moody was so impressed by his performance as the Pope in a play about Galileo that he asked the company's leading actor, Joseph O'Connor, what he thought of him. He said: 'I think we have a wonderful character actor who can give whatever weight and authority you need to any part.'

O'Connor and O'Toole, Irish blood brothers, although separated by a generation in years, became close friends. Together they would talk about the future. Peter had one idea in his mind that was unalterable. 'He would say,' O'Connor recalls, ' "When I get to the top . . ." using the phrase without any conceit at all. It was as if he were saying, "When I get to Liverpool". It was a matter of inevitability. He was travelling and the destination was the top. There was never any doubt in his mind about it.

'He had talent and extraordinary good looks—although the beauty of his face was never in his features. It was the beauty of the life that was in it—and the imagination that you saw working in it.'

O'Toole's career blossomed and burgeoned in Bristol, then one of the few provincial centres of good theatre left in Britain. In the last decade, theatres have established themselves in a number of British cities. In the fifties, Bristol was almost unique.

By most of his actions at the theatre, Peter showed his innate respect for what the Bristol Old Vic represented. There were no arguments with directors—a boast that he would not be able to make in the years to come. Joe O'Connor recalled: 'It was delicate guidance that he required anyway—not direction.'

Since those days he has said he owes everything to Bristol—'the loveliest theatre in the world, a little jewel box'. For one thing, it confirmed that he was right in choosing the stage for a career. 'If I hadn't become an actor,' he said once, 'I probably would have been a criminal. Once I made the decision to act, I knew I'd have to do it better than any man or woman alive. Otherwise I'd never be able to get out of bed.'

Bristol more than helped Peter O'Toole get out of bed. John Coë, at the time theatre critic for the Bristol *Evening*

Post, remembers Peter's performance as the tramp Vladimir in *Waiting for Godot* as one of the most exciting experiences he ever had. And *The Times's* critic described it as one of the most astonishing performances ever seen in such a young actor. 'He was one of the people who brought a great deal of authority to the Bristol Old Vic and made it one of the most important repertory theatres in the land, says Coë.'

It was hard work being part of a busy, prestigious repertory company. Speeches were long and had to be not merely learned and understood, but developed and interpreted. And two sets of speeches had to be prepared simultaneously, those for the play currently being presented and the ones for the play that would follow. And sometimes, there were preliminary readings of the play that would come after that one.

There wasn't much time to socialise. But Peter made that time. Life was to be lived and he was determined to use it for that purpose. He knew people in the city and found out where the action was. If there was a drinking party among the local intelligentsia, there was a good chance that Peter would be there swilling beer with the crowd. There were bawdy songs to croak, or poetry to recite, or girls to woo. He enjoyed it all tremendously.

Because he couldn't afford to buy all the drink he wanted, he learned how to manufacture it. 'The way I make rhubarb wine, it's got a kick like an ox,' he says. 'Potent as hell.'

He supervised his own highly illegal Peter O'Toole Distilliary. The only problem was finding somewhere to store the hooch, including a particularly lethal form of whisky. In the end some huge carboys were found, the ones used for the storage of acid. As he has said, judging by the taste of the brew, the containers couldn't have been washed out quite as well as they should. But he was rarely drunk any more. Or at least drinking never prevented him doing his work properly.

Joe O'Connor told me of several parties with home-made mead, which used to send people rather wild. There was one in particular that he remembered vividly. 'His sister, Pat, was down in Bristol and we had a party for her. Afterwards, at about one o'clock in the morning, we were in the street where we met a policeman who said something rather offensive to us. Mercifully, his sister hit the policeman before Peter did.'

But sometimes, Peter's friends worried about the company he kept. Nat Brenner says: 'He cultivated the friendship of people who were plainly psychopathic. They were physically dangerous to him, but somehow they had a fascination for him. Particularly if the person was an artist of some kind, but a little bit—shall we say—ill.' He would meet them in one of the local pubs where he seemed as much a fixture as the levers used for pulling the pints. One of his closest friends was George Sims, who ran the Naval Volunteer in King Street, a popular sawdust-strewn hostelry that prided itself on serving the best Bass and Guinness in Bristol, if not further afield, too. It was a marvellous hard-drinking man's pub, in which women were the subject of many a conversation but, apart from a barmaid showing a considerable amount of cleavage, they were rarely seen in person. It was an atmosphere that Peter found enticingly exciting.

As Joe O'Connor recalled: 'He loved argument. So did I, but he was a very contentious arguer. There were a lot of things we disagreed about, and I remember once at a party he said, "Do you sometimes feel like hitting me?" I said, "Yes." Whereupon he put his arms around me and hugged me—which, on the whole, was rather untypical of the man.'

The two men would argue about religion and politics. O'Connor would try to explain the reasons for his being a practising Catholic, while O'Toole would stick to his guns as a 'retired Christian'. It was easier to discuss politics. It was the time of Suez, and Peter regarded the British Government's invasion of Egypt as an affront to himself as well as to civilisation. He was angry, the sort of anger that took a considerable amount of liquid to quell.

Once that excitement was inside him, going home to sleep was a seemingly unnecessary waste of time. Frank Finlay told me of the occasion when he himself was in Bristol staying at the local YMCA. He was part of an impoverished band of itinerant players doing a series of one-night stands. O'Toole got to hear that his old RADA chum was in town and decided to pay him a visit. The only problem was that it was the middle of the night and the YMCA was locked up.

Peter's solution to the problem was simply to climb through the window—even though it was four storeys up. Fortified by the night's supply of liquor, the long O'Toole legs shinned their way up the window ledges of the lower floors and found themselves outside Finlay's room.

'Open up,' called Peter affecting much more of an Irish accent than was usual.

'What the hell are you doin' here?' At which point, Frank opened the window and Peter climbed in, bottle in hand.

Brenner would tell him to be cautious. Once, he turned up at the stage door, shaken, dirty and bruised. It was clear he'd been in a fight. 'Why do you do this to yourself?' the director asked him. 'Why do you court this kind of trouble?'

Peter replied: 'I need it. I need to feed on it in order to inform myself about these people.'

It was as though he were already preparing himself for *Lawrence of Arabia*. So much of his behaviour was like the disturbed Lawrence, trying to live a life that was so difficult, other people would probably regard it as impossible.

There were times when Brenner would get a call from the local hospital. 'We have a Mr O'Toole here, asking for you,' reported a nurse. 'He came in here complaining about pains in the head.'

Once, just before a matinée, Peter was rushed to the X-ray room and then pulled out of the hospital by Brenner so that he could do the show before the results were known. He was willing to be seen by the hospital, but not to await the diagnosis or take time over the treatment.

'He was plainly self-destructive in whatever he did. Yet there was also a sense of vitality, of knowing that life is for the living.'

His drinking was prodigious, and on more than one occasion he found himself in collision with the local constabulary. Like the time he wrapped himself and a second-hand car around a city lamppost. Or another time when he knocked down a bollard in Whiteladies Road. When a policeman shouted at him to remember the side of the road on which he was supposed to drive, he shouted back: 'Yes—and keep the Pope off the moon!'

Another time, he succeeded in driving the car down a sweep of steps like a character in *Bullitt*. His reputation as a driver had preceeded him. When he was due to take his driving test in Bristol, the examiner looked out at the icy road and was delighted to call it off. Later, he was to write off both a Riley and an MG. In fact, when he crashed one car after falling asleep at the wheel on the M1, he didn't even bother to collect the resultant hunk of twisted metal.

Before long, he lost his driving licence and decided not to drive again. He was prepared to give no such undertaking about drinking, or about another passion he developed while in the city—cricket.

He played on Sundays for a local scratch XI. 'Quite a neat bowler and batsman,' recalls John Coë, who played for the press. 'Not up to county standard, but very good.'

The only trouble was that he tended to regard the umpire as though he were a director, and to be given Out was to be treated like an amateur in a turn-of-the-century vaudeville theatre subjected to the indignity of the hook which dragged him off stage.

'Absolute rubbish, umpire,' he would call, faced with that irreversible monosyllabic word. 'I couldn't possibly be Out.' The argument would go on, enlivening for the spectators what had been perhaps a less than entertaining day. 'I was playing the ball which made contact.'

He would drag up any excuse available to him. He needed to be part of the action. 'He couldn't see himself spending five hours sitting on his bottom waiting in the pavilion,' Coë recalls. And he would tell the team captain: 'I don't want to field. I want to bo-w-l.' The way he pronounced it, he could have been referring to his lower intestines.

Of course, it was a great opportunity to get his revenge on the gentlemen of the press. Give him a chance to bo-w-l, and there was an inevitable shout of 'Howzzat?' Unless the umpire stuck up his finger, there appeared the instant risk of mayhem at the wicket. Afterwards, there would be a beer in the clubhouse. A fun afternoon had ended and Peter had had his slice of the action.

In Bristol, he shared a flat with another actor. When they gave the place up, he walked out of the house with all his belongings in a small suitcase. His friend needed a van. But it wasn't a time for accumulating possessions, although the twenty pounds a week Peter earned seemed like big money at the end of the fifties. It was all that professional footballers were allowed to earn.

He was to be in Bristol for three years, during which he played no fewer than seventy-nine roles, playing one, learning another, changing on average once every four weeks. *Volpone*—in which he played Corvino—was followed by the role of the Duke of Cornwall in *King Lear*. He played Lodovico in *Othello* at the time he was rehearsing as Baron Parsnip for Bristol's *Sleeping Beauty* pantomime—a lovely bit of British theatrical tradition, it not only brought in a different, and on the whole younger, set of customers, it also broadened the actors' experience and served to reduce any conceit which the haughtier plains of classical theatre may have given them.

He was greatly influenced by the people working with him. Eric Porter he remembers with the greatest admiration—both as *King Lear* and as the dame in *Dick Whittington*. 'Eric was one of the two great Lears I've seen,' he once told John Walker in *The Observer*—the other was Donald Wolfit. 'He was the best young actor I'd ever seen, a real catalyst for me. Eric was similar to me in all sorts of ways. He released a lot of my own energies because of his great looseness and power.'

It was a marvellous time for Peter. He played in London for the first time—in July 1949 as Peter Shirley in Shaw's

Major Barbara. In a way it was a homecoming. He was back on the same stage where he had had his audition just a year before. Bristol had taken over the main Old Vic for a short season and Peter O'Toole was one of the bright spots in their programme.

In his second full year, the arena widened still further. Bristol appeared to like Peter O'Toole and its Old Vic company backed the opinions of the audiences. John Coë put it to me like this: 'Everthing he touched was endowed with this intuitive insight into what he was creating. He lacked the discipline that one expected from someone who was aiming for the top of his profession. But he was naturally endowed with good looks, an excellent figure, just the right height—and a voice which many women who are inveterate theatregoers in Bristol would say charmed the birds out of the trees.'

Years later, Peter told an interviewer: 'At the Bristol Old Vic, I used to set the house on fire with ten-minute parts. Had them all clapping me like mad. Time after time, I did it! But then I played lead parts. You can't set the house on fire for two and a half hours.' In actual fact, he did. He was clearly an actor of exceptional diversity and talent. In a matter of weeks, he was Mr Jaggers in a dramatised version of *Great Expectations* and Alfred Doolittle in *Pygmalion.* He was Lysander in *A Midsummer Night's Dream* and then the angry young man personified, Jimmy Porter, in *Look Back In Anger,* John Osborne's play which, fresh from its run at the Royal Court, was still the most talked about work in the contemporary British theatre. There were also the parts of the Angel in *Sodom and Gomorrah,* the General in Peter Ustinov's *Romanoff and Juliet* and Mrs Millie Baba in *Ali Baba and the Forty Thieves.* It was a notable event for him. In between acts, he served icecream—he even sold one to an expatriate Bristolian in the city to visit his mother, Cary Grant.

In July 1957, he had the lead role of the sick Uncle Gustave in *Oh, Mein Papa.* Artistically, it wasn't much, but it was a milestone. The company was invited to take the play to London, which was not merely a compliment to the players but provided the opportunity of money for Bristol of a kind that could only come from the commercial theatre. As far as Peter was concerned, there were strings fairly tightly attached. Brenner refused to allow him to stay in London for more than three months. 'It was in his interest and ours but mainly in his, because he still needed to get more classical rep under his belt.'

If he worried about this, he didn't show it. Neither would there have been any cause for concern. The play opened at the Garrick to less than overwhelming critical acclaim and barely lasted the three months that had worried the people at Bristol so much. Not even the duet that Peter sang with Rachel Roberts enchanted audiences very much.

On the first night, the players were booed off the stage. Peter slunk out of the theatre and got drunk. He was found by a policeman leaning up against a wall in Holborn and spent the night in Bow Street police station. He told the magistrate next morning—who fined him five pounds—that he had been 'celebrating' on mead.

In fact, O'Toole was philosophical about *Oh, Mein Papa*. He said it didn't matter and gave the impression that it really didn't, as if it were a necessary struggle prior to success. It was a flop, but it was the West End and had represented stardom of a sort, the kind for which Peter and the other aspirants at that Old Vic audition would have been grateful to exchange a month's supply of luncheon vouchers. And this ability of Peter's to take things as they came was almost as widely talked about as his performances. His reaction to *Papa* became a topic of discussion in a drama class at Cardiff University. An instructor declared: 'This old man of sixty or seventy, this Peter O'Toole who is never going to make it big . . . isn't it a delight when you can find someone who clearly shows no bitterness or resentment!' And he meant it.

Harold Hobson was later to describe Peter as a 'very old-fashioned actor'. Strange, paradoxical—considering the vibrancy that seemed to infect his roustabout behaviour—but true. He was flamboyant, larger than life, as though in some ways emulating the actor-managers of old. Like them, too, he always knew just how good he was. But to his credit, he was equally always ready to learn. If old habits die hard, the one he picked up at RADA about learning not just the lines of his speeches but also the background of every role, the history of the period in which the play was set, wouldn't go away, and he showed it in his work.

All that, naturally enough, leaves an impression of his being nothing if not the supreme professional. There were other characteristics that give a different insight into his personality. His respect for directors—and their direction—was sometimes minimal. A wink, a nod, a casual refusal to follow an instruction through, left no doubt that there were times when he felt certain he knew a great deal more about a play than the directors did.

Was it entirely professional to arrive at 10.45 for a 10 a.m. rehearsal? His colleagues at Bristol didn't think so. John Coë remembers him being told that he wouldn't last a week at Joan Littlewood's Theatre Workshop if his standards of punctuality operated there. But it wasn't prima donna behaviour either. He didn't expect the show to wait for him and then to be greeted with deferential bows and curtseys on arrival. He knew he was in the wrong—and usually had what he believed to be a perfect excuse to explain his behaviour.

Those excuses grew more and more implausible as the occasions increased in number. The more implausible the excuse, the more he expected people to believe him—which came to be recognised as typical O'Toole behaviour. 'I expected to be called at nine o'clock, but the man who promised to call me didn't turn up. I had a late night last night, you know how it is. It isn't the sort of thing, I usually want to do, old chap.'

It didn't help in endearing him to the management. Warren-Jenkins, who was a guest director at Bristol, complained vociferously to Nat Brenner. 'This man's behaviour is disgraceful. A young actor like he ought to be sacked—or horse whipped.'

He was never late for a performance, but his standard of punctuality for rehearsals left much to be desired. To be fair, he was not being deliberately difficult. He was wracked with the problem that would be with him into middle age, acute insomnia. He would go to bed at night with the lines of the play he had been performing a few short hours before running circles around his brain. And if not the lines of the play, the ones recited to him by a girlfriend, or the jokes he told and heard over a succession of pints of beer or glasses of whisky. When sleep did come in the early hours of the morning it was all powerful, enveloping his mind as heavily as the blanket on the bed enveloped his body. As one friend told me: 'He would go to bed at night and then die.'

Sometimes he crept into rehearsals, not so much hoping to avoid a scene but because he genuinely felt ashamed. 'Peter,' says Brenner, 'is a living example of Einstein's theory on relativity and time. He was always moving so fast that he lost time in the middle. He cared deeply.'

Finally, the company had to find someone to get him up in the morning. They chose the man who was normally employed as the city's rat-catcher. He took his Morris Minor van to O'Toole's lodgings and there he would bang on the door until the actor was forced out of bed to open it. When even that failed to work, Peter was persuaded to part with a key to the room. It was easy from then on. The rat-catcher simply walked in and pulled him out of bed. When his 'charge' was difficult, he pulled harder. On more than one occasion, he used his fists. Peter did turn up for rehearsal on time, but often with a red eye that was rapidly changing to blue.

If he did nothing else in 1958, he made the mark that separated him from all the journeyman actors who make successful enough careers out of encouraging audiences to believe every line they recite either on stage or before a movie or TV camera. He played *Hamlet* and his interpretation of the Prince of Denmark changed everything. It was a *Hamlet* with a beard—'why should Hamlet be the only bloke in Elsinore with a razor?' he asked.

Joe O'Connor said: 'I'll always remember the way he greeted Horatio, Marcellus and Bernardo when they came to tell him about the ghost. He made each phrase fit the hierarchy of the friendship. He greeted each as an equal—the true character of an aristocrat. But Horatio was greeted as an old friend, Marcellus, as a man he knew and respected and Bernardo whom he hardly knew at all.'

People watching his performance on the first night said they had seen nothing like it before. The next day the London critics confirmed the judgment. The *Daily Telegraph,* however, was a little unsure. The paper's headline gives the impression that the sub-editor who wrote it realised he was recording an important piece of theatrical history: '24-Year-Old as Hamlet', but then went on to say 'Performance Lacks Nobility'.

Patrick Gibbs wrote: 'The *Hamlet* given by the Bristol Old Vic in the Theatre Royal here tonight had in the name part, Peter O'Toole, a young actor little known to the world at large but much talked about in theatrical circles recently as very promising.

'Gielgud has said an actor should get his first *Hamlet* over before the age of thirty. Mr O'Toole does so with, I understand, six years to spare and gives by any standards a performance remarkable for coherence. It is also completely without sense of strain.'

But then came the part when he justified the headline. 'No great moments resulted. Not for instance in the scenes with the Ghost, Gertrude or the Players in which many Hamlets make their mark—although each was well enough played. That excitement was lacking was due, I think, to the actor's appearance. With curly wig, a curious beard and unhelpful costume, he put me in mind of an Italian barber. His Hamlet lacked nobility.' But that didn't put off potential audiences. Everyone else seemed to think he was superb. But he remained modest about the achievement. 'I was protected as much as possible and the play was cut to suit my capabilities,' he said once.

From all over the country, theatre enthusiasts and fellow actors who were either not working or could take time off to attend a matinée, came and stayed long enough to cheer, or to pound his back in his dressing room afterwards. There was no finer compliment for any actor. For a twenty-five year-old who always knew it would be just a matter of time before he got to the top, it was sweetness indeed.

Peter Hall, about to become the head of the Shakespeare Memorial Theatre at Stratford-on-Avon, saw this Hamlet, too. 'It was rough hewn,' said Sir Peter, now in charge of the National Theatre, 'sometimes the words weren't said exactly right and the metre was not always perfect. But it was marvellous. I could see then the sparks of genius—and that isn't using too fine a word.'

Kenneth Tynan said that with Peter's perception of the role, he deserved to be at the very top of his profession.

It wasn't the only mark of recognition. That year, the Bristol University Drama Society elected Peter as their honorary president. They said they saw in him the personification of their own ambitions. He was not just a brilliant actor and interpreter of the theatre. He was young, and clearly sufficiently rebellious to commend himself to all that they thought important in life.

But ask him what his favourite roles were then, and he will tell you the comedies—particularly Doolittle in *Pygmalion*.

There were some Bristolians who didn't appreciate him quite so much. When he played a teddy boy in *The Pier,* the local teds thought he had gone over the top somewhat. They didn't like the realism of his performance—and told him so as they stood outside the stage door, bicycle chains in hand.

At the end of three years, it was clearly time for him to go. He had done enough—even the Bristol Old Vic had to admit that one of their current principal assets would only be blocking his career by staying there any longer.

55

Peter wasn't always in the best of health. He had had his share of illness as a child—numerous eye operations, a bout of TB and peritonitis—all kept him away from school. But trouble with his eyes persisted and now he was developing cysts over the cornea, a difficulty that would plague him frequently. He went into Charing Cross Hospital, only to insist on leaving his bed to see his friend James Villiers in the play *Tomorrow With Feeling* at the Duke of York's Theatre. The doctors said no, but Peter went just the same. 'He told me he just wanted to see his mate—and then say, "Thank you, Jimbo" after it was over,' Villiers recalled for me. 'I thought that was terrific.'

Perhaps that was predictable behaviour for an actor already listed with Trevor Howard, Peter Finch, and the thirsty Irish dramatist, Brendan Behan, as one of the Hell Raisers of 1959. That was Peter Evans's assessment in the London *Daily Express*. He was in tremendous demand. Hardly a week went by when there wasn't an invitation to join one company or another. The offer he accepted was to tour in a production of a play called *The Holiday*.

It was a very important move for Peter's private life. In the cast was a very pretty young Welsh actress called Sian Phillips.

Five

IT WAS A relationship that they kept mostly to themselves at the beginning of 1959. Everyone knew that Peter still had an eye for the ladies and it seemed quite the reasonable thing for him to show an interest in the prettiest and most talented girl in the cast, the twenty-five-year-old girl from Gwan-cae-Gur-wen, who was the daughter of a retired policeman.

But both decided to keep it quiet for the time being. There were reasons. For one thing, Peter was on the verge of what already seemed like being a brilliant career and neither of them wanted to detract from that. For another, Sian was already married, although she had separated from her Scottish university lecturer husband for four years.

From Cardiff University she had graduated with honours in English and worked for a time as a BBC Welsh Region announcer. Then she went to RADA—although after Peter had been there—and won the gold medal.

She and Peter were first seen in public, holding hands and calling each other 'darling', at the August 1959 Eisteddfod in Cardiff. She was a white-robed druid taking part in the chairing of the Bard.

Her first ever stage appearance had been in a RADA production of Ibsen's *Hedda Gabler*. The critics who saw it were enchanted.

Which was more than any of them were with *The Holiday*. Sian has said: 'It was a terrible play and we knew it never had the chance of getting to London. We stayed with it just to be together.' And it was true they both loved being with each

57

other. They played brother and sister on stage, but off stage their relationship was very different. The play went to Birmingham, Nottingham, Leeds, Scotland—all promised as part of a pre-London run. In Scotland it fizzled out. But Peter already had the chance of the lead part in a new angry-young-man-type drama at London's Royal Court Theatre. The play was called *The Long And The Short And The Tall,* and both Sian and Peter were very excited about it. Neither, however, could have had any notion of quite how important the play would be for him.

He was cast as an angry young soldier, Private Bamforth, in the play by Willis Hall (who hailed from the same area of Leeds as himself) which took its title from a well-known World War II song. It had first been put on at the previous year's Edinburgh Festival by the amateur Oxford Theatre Group and this was its first professional production.

The Long And The Short And The Tall was instantly acclaimed, and Peter became a nationally-known star. If it is the lot of all great men to struggle and suffer before hitting it big, Peter's share of both struggling and suffering was incredibly and mercifully short.

Alan Dent, in the respected London paper, *News Chronicle,* described the play about a lost patrol surrounded by Japanese in the steaming jungles of Malaya as 'the best anti-war play since *Journey's End'*. Robert Shaw and Ronald Fraser were both singled out for praise, but it was Peter O'Toole who was at the top of every critic's list. Dent called his portrayal of the insubordinate private soldier 'outstanding'.

In the *Sunday Times,* Harold Hobson recalled what he had said of him in Bristol. 'Is Mr O'Toole too exuberant at the start?' he asked. 'Perhaps. But then I don't like bawdy jokes'—a reference to the way the company of seven British soldiers just before the fall of Singapore keep each other amused with dirty stories. 'But he is the point of active life in the play, and to the piece's unexpected and beautiful lyric passage in the second act, he supplies a subdued musical

58

accompaniment or comment, traditional, ribald and ironic which is not easy to be forgotten.'

Of course, he was helped by the play, by the writer, and by Lindsay Anderson who directed. But Peter's performance during its run stood up on its own sufficiently strongly to earn him the London Critic's Award for Best Actor of the Year. Not most promising newcomer—but best actor. He had arrived. And in lights.

It was a great time for him, acting on stage in the evening, followed by performing in a pub or two. His favourites, when he could get a taxi there in time, were the Salisbury and Cranbourne in the heart of theatreland. The rest of the time he spent in the company of people like Richard Harris, Daniel Massey, James Villiers and the agent Peter Crouch. People who witnessed those sessions of verbal repartee and plenty of booze by a roaring fire will not forget them in a hurry.

Sometimes he wasn't all that successful in his entertainment habits. Donald Pleasence recalled for me the night when he, Peter and Robert Shaw tried to go to the restaurant above the Royal Court. Peter, star of the play downstairs, wasn't allowed in. He didn't have a tie. Which shows how long ago 1959 was.

But the run was not trouble free. More than once—and to the great annoyance of Mr Anderson—Peter arrived at the theatre just as his understudy was due to go on. He even turned up once wearing a grey top hat and tails, with only three minutes to spare before curtain up. He had been stranded by fog in Birmingham where he had been attending the wedding of his sister Pat to a future Member of Parliament. It was January and he was frightened of driving back. In the end, he chartered a plane for two hundred pounds and ordered the pilot to Heathrow—which was shut by fog, too. He landed at Blackbushe, a small private airfield south-west of London, and hired a fast car to get him to the Sloane Square theatre.

Anderson, who already had a reputation as the angriest

young director-producer in Britain, was justifying his title. 'I'm furious,' he said. 'I've never known anything quite so monstrously unprofessional.'

Peter was unrepentant. 'I've never missed an entrance or cue yet. We'll have to kiss and make up.' When things like that did happen to him, there was usually an important personal reason for it.

Frank Finlay once called at the Royal Court dressing room during the run of the play and couldn't see any sign of Peter or any of his fellow actors. Time was gushing more than just rushing out, and still no sign of life. Finlay sat in the star dressing-room and heard the call boy shout 'Beginners'—but Peter O'Toole was quite obviously not ready to begin yet. There were perhaps two minutes to go when a dishevelled Peter burst into the dressing-room holding a steaming plate of sausages, eggs and beans which he was pushing into his mouth.

'Hello, Frank,' he said. 'You know what, I'm in love!'

Frank told him he was delighted, only to be interrupted by another knock from the call boy.

'Peter . . .' said Finlay, motioning to the door.

'Bugger that,' said O'Toole. 'I tell you I'm in love.' And as he put on his make-up, still shovelling baked beans into his mouth, he told him about the girl of his dreams—Sian.

In December 1959, they announced their marriage. Sian told the press: 'Peter and I would have loved to announce our romance with a fanfare of trumpets, but there were difficulties.' And Peter added: 'We wanted to live a normal life out of the headlines, in peace.'

The main difficulty had been Sian's first marriage. But now there was another one—which in 1959 still made people in the public eye act carefully and guardedly. Sian was pregnant. They had married in Dublin, and ever since then, both Peter and Sian have gone out of their way to stress that neither of them can remember the date of the ceremony—or the place.

Neither of their parents were present, although both fathers said they were delighted with the news. The announcement followed their first BBC TV play together, *The King's Daughter*. Appropriately, they played lovers although none of the rest of the cast had realised how true to life the theme had been.

Three months later, in March 1960, their daughter Kate was born. They said they named her after Katharine Hepburn. Connie and Patty came to London to meet their grandchild and 'wet' the baby's head. After everyone else had gone to bed, Peter and his father stayed up drinking. Eventually, O'Toole junior was out—lying on the floor; and, as he has since said, not so much asleep as 'crucified'. His father, however, still had room for more. He left the room to get another bottle. When he returned, he tried to wake Peter. 'Come on, son,' he called. 'On yer feet. On yer feet.' But Peter didn't want to get on his feet—or if he did, there was nothing he could do about it. Patty was intelligent enough to realise that. 'OK,' he said, 'I can't lift yer. So I'll have to join yer. Move up . . .' He then lay by Peter's side and father and son fell asleep: kindred spirits as always.

It was a time when success had begun to drive O'Toole towards making the very mistake he had sworn at RADA he would never do. He was playing checkers with his career; not merely acting on the stage and television, but planning to go into films and to make them himself, starring other people.

That was ambition indeed for a twenty-six year-old, but already he and Sian had registered a company to do just that. They called it Keep Films Ltd—'keep' meaning 'I keep what I earn and don't give it to anyone else.' To make sure that the operation was run profitably, he had American producer Jules Buck in tow as a full partner acting as his business adviser.

Buck had been impressed with Peter's work from the time he saw him in a small TV role while still at Bristol. Now he was there to guide his career, suggesting changes in his approach to the business of being an actor. Some of the changes were small. Some Peter disagreed with. But one was vital. Buck asked him: 'Do you just want to become a successful actor or do you want to be an international star?'

'Jules,' Peter replied, 'I want in.'

'Right,' said Buck. 'You'd better have a nose job.' Peter took the advice—and that 'magnificent' nose admired so much by his fellow students at RADA was trimmed appreciably.

'Oh, what a sacrifice,' Roy Kinnear only half jokes. 'What a sacrifice! Never has a nose given so much . . .'

He had, in fact, now made his film debut—that is, if you didn't count all those times he broke limbs stunting for other people. He had a day's work, mostly playing the bagpipes, in Robert Stevenson's production of his namesake's story, *Kidnapped*. Stevenson said at the time, 'I predict he will make a very important mark within five years.'

He had a much bigger role in a worthy but heavy movie called *The Savage Innocents,* starring Anthony Quinn. In a way, it was only half an O'Toole performance. His voice was dubbed. The reason, Peter has gone on record as saying, was that he considered the dialogue literally unspeakable. Robert Rietty, the actor who spoke the lines, told me that the producer Maleno Malenotti's misguided reason was that he didn't think the O'Toole voice sounded masculine enough.

Producers have found themselves on the wrong side of reason when dealing with Peter quite a few times since then. Sam Spiegel, for instance, had been recommended to give him a screentest. It was not an auspicious meeting with the man who was to play a vital part in Peter's career.

The part he was given was of a doctor in a hospital ward. Peter decided to provide his own dialogue. 'It's all right, Mrs Spiegel,' he said looking into the camera while the producer squirmed. 'But your son will never play the violin again.'

The two men did not meet again for another year. As Peter once admitted in an interview with *Esquire* magazine, he has always been prone to working hard to build up something important—only to knock it down again 'just for the hell of it'. He was not overly concerned, however. It seemed that films were going to be no more than a mere sideline to the much more important career he was singling out for himself as a Shakespearean actor.

Peter Hall, at thirty-six already established as one of Britain's greatest theatrical producers, had invited Peter to join the Shakespeare Memorial Theatre Company at Stratford-on-Avon. It was an invitation that seemed to Peter in those early days of 1960 to be roughly equivalent to an accolade. If *The Long And The Short And The Tall* had earned him the recognition of the critics, being invited to play at Stratford was a tribute from his peers at an age when he felt he not only deserved it, but could also handle it.

It was what he wanted above all else—although his whole career could have taken a totally different route had he gone along with another film idea. He was asked if he would like to play opposite Elizabeth Taylor in *Cleopatra*. He said, yes, of course he would. It was the chance of international stardom at the click of a camera shutter—except that no one could say when filming would begin and Peter wanted desperately to go to Stratford. The part of Mark Antony went instead to Richard Burton—and everyone knows what happened as a result of that. Had things been different, Elizabeth Taylor might just have had a celebrated divorce or two from Peter O'Toole. But his career was moving ahead just the same.

His third movie, *The Day They Robbed The Bank Of England,* in which he played a young guards officer, came out at about the time he arrived at Stratford. It was a portent of things to come. John Le Mesurier, one of Britain's leading character actors who was also in the film, told me: 'He was marvellous. Even then, he was full of ideas of how he wanted to play the part. There was no heavy stuff from him at all. In fact, we thought he was very pleasant—and very, very good.'

Readers of the London *Evening News* were told: 'It happened again this week—that magical moment in the critic's routine when a magnetic spark seems to come out of the screen and he knows that he is seeing the birth of a great star.

'It comes too seldom these days. And often the spark of life dies out through neglect or bad use by the producers. But I have an idea that Peter O'Toole is going to blaze a fiery trail over our screens that will make some other reigning satellites look pale . . .

'What are O'Toole's qualities that convince me about his future? First, that essential air of being in charge. Great stars always have that happy knack of seeming to be alive in a dead world of photographed celluloid. Next, his square-round face which will do for a variety of parts.' These were prescient words indeed. But for the moment films were going to have to wait.

On 14 April 1960, Peter Evans was to ask in the *Daily Express:* 'Is this the next Olivier?' Praise came no higher.

The day before, Bernard Levin, a man who could already slaughter careers with a few choice sentences, had described Peter's performance in *The Merchant Of Venice* at Stratford as a 'radiant masterpiece'.

The response from people who had witnessed that 'masterpiece' was said to be even greater than that which had greeted Richard Burton's triumph there, a few years before.

Peter played Shylock, giving his own, novel interpretation to the role—and wearing a totally new putty nose. If only he had waited for the plastic surgery! Nevertheless, he managed exceedingly well without it.

He had formed the role to his own making. He read books on Jewish law and traditions for five weeks before going into rehearsal, and then discussed the play with a lecturer in English at Cardiff University, Dr Moelwyn Merchant, an appropriate enough name. In the end, his Shylock wasn't the cringing moneylender of so many previous interpretations, but a younger, more determined man. He found his own ways of conveying the personality of the merchant—not simply in the words or the way he said them, or even in the gestures which can be so important in the role. It was more the mechanics of those gestures. Shylock would have to rend his garments—the traditional Jewish expression of mourning. Peter ordered the costume designer to construct his doublet specially, so that it would crackle through the house as the act of rending proceeded. 'It was marvellous,' recalled O'Connor. 'The silence broken by that marvellous sound.'

Bringing him to Stratford had been all Peter Hall's idea, inspired by the performance of *Hamlet* he had seen at Bristol. From the moment O'Toole arrived at the Memorial Theatre, Hall knew it had been a wise choice—although, as he told me, 'I had engaged a man with a wonderfully big hooter, which I thought was one of his greatest assets. And this chap arrives with a really tiny nose. I didn't know anything about it until he turned up for rehearsals with it. Nevertheless, I knew immediately we had made the discovery of a very major actor in classical roles, which would be of great use to our whole enterprise.'

That fact became clear on the first night, the night that Joe O'Connor says was 'one of the most marvellous events in the history of the theatre. I knew then he was the Crown Prince of the classical stage.'

Peter had been physically sick before going on stage—a situation that was not new. He often vomited before a performance, sweating so copiously that he could be seen wiping his hands on his clothes in the wings before his entrance.

'The emotion,' wrote Levin 'comes from the range of Mr Peter O'Toole's incomparable reading of Shylock. He makes the Jew a figure of implacable enmity, but swayed by feelings incomprehensible to those around him.

'This is a man for whom sympathy comes in Mr O'Toole's reading, not the easy way of a sob or a whine, but the deep, sure way of a round, full portrayal of a man whose primitive gods will give him no rest.'

But Levin was not uncritical of the performance, even so. 'Mr O'Toole's deep and moving and true Shylock is marred by the imposition of a foolish, inaccurate, unnecessary, obtrusive, vulgar, distasteful mock-Yiddish accent.' That was telling him. Nevertheless, within a year, Levin was singling out that performance of *The Merchant* as being one of the most memorable in his experience. He said the play was 'a torrent of wit and passion and beauty, containing such trophies for the mantelpiece of memory as Mr Peter O'Toole's implacably pitiful Shylock'.

In the London *Evening News,* David Wainwright wrote: 'As Shylock, Peter O'Toole—hitherto known as a tough young man in war plays—rose magnificently to his opportunity. He looked superb, a dignified figure from the New Testament, rather than the Old, a Christ in torment. Every anguished twist of the fingers, every jerk of tension when anyone touched him, were illuminating.'

His performance was well complemented by Dorothy Tutin's Portia, but it was O'Toole's play all the way. And as a gesture to this Crown Prince, Dorothy Tutin let everyone know what she thought at the curtain call. She moved over to Peter and took his hand. Nat Brenner was moved by the sight. 'It showed enormous respect for an impressive young actor,' he said.

It had unquestionably made him a big star, capable, if he wished it, of commanding a fortune. His life had jumped into a new gear.

It was a moment of glory for the family. Connie O'Toole travelled from Leeds to be there to witness what she knew would be her son's triumph, and couldn't get a seat. She had to be content to stand at the back of the theatre. She deliberately didn't tell Peter she was coming. 'I wanted him to act without knowing I was in the audience,' she explained. It was an illuminating statement. Despite all that had happened to him in the years since his childhood—the newspaper, the navy, RADA, Bristol—he was still exceedingly influenced by his parents, still wanted their approval.

But now he had Sian and baby Kate to think about, too. He was totally overwhelmed that night at Stratford. The make-up was taken off in a daze and he embraced Sian and kissed Kate gently on the cheek. And then he disappeared. No one knew where he was going. He was away for several hours. 'I went searching for that haystack,' he told Sian when he got back to the apartment they had rented in Stratford for the season. 'The dungheap. It's not far from here at all.' The moment of success was also one for reflection.

The Merchant changed Peter. That day, a member of the company recalled for me twenty-two years later, he became a different man. The diffidence and the nerves were now muted. From the second night, he could no longer be seen wringing his hands, wiping the sweat on his doublet. He was a much more assured man—and, perhaps just a little less concerned about the other members of the company, perhaps a little more arrogant.

He was also plainly a genius, although there are those who say that with those nerves vanished some of the brilliance. Nevertheless, his Petruchio in Stratford's next production, *The Taming of the Shrew,* was outstanding—again played with his own very individual interpretation. The production became something of a family affair. The play's Kate, Peggy Ashcroft, brought on Peter's own Kate at the end of the performance.

Elizabeth Sellars, who had appeared with him in *The Day They Robbed The Bank Of England,* as well as playing Bianca in *The Taming of the Shrew* and Thersites in *Troilus And Cressida,* has only the happiest memories of those days. He was warm and friendly; joined in all the fun, mostly settled around the favourite Stratford 'local', the Dirty Duck. Ben Shepherd, the landlord, was, he said, 'the patron saint of us all'. Situated down by the river it was everyone's most popular haunt. For more than a year Peter held the Dirty Duck's speed record for consuming the yard of ale—forty seconds. Several years later, he tried to equal it and confessed he no longer had the stamina. Certainly there were fights; undoubtedly there was an inordinate amount of drinking. As Peter once said: 'People treat Stratford as a place for pilgrimage, like Lourdes or Bethlehem. But there's nothing else to do there except drink. The locals detest the actors.'

When Elizabeth married her surgeon husband, Frank Henley, Peter went to the reception in the little village of Broad Camden. He was literally the life and soul of the party.

Peter was obviously at home at Stratford. Early in his career there, he and another player went into a local café, ordered a huge meal which they thoroughly enjoyed—and then ran out. For months, both of them avoided the place as though it had a cross proclaiming yellow fever painted on its door. But later in the year he went back, ordered another meal, and not only paid for it but left an exorbitant tip.

The mere fact of being at Stratford was enough for Peter. He was earning forty-five pounds a week, a fair salary for the time, but that was not important. He had been offered a chance to go to Hollywood to make a new version of the Kipling Story, *Kim,* and turned it down flat. A Broadway manager wanted him to play the lead in *Macbeth.* He said no, he wanted his Shakespeare neat, and in the place where it seemed most right to play him.

O'Toole was always the company man. He didn't demand superstar treatment at Stratford. There were no requests for improved dressing room facilities, for valets or other forms of pampering. He was in the company of great professionals and he thrived on such stimulation. Patrick Wymark and Max Adrian were in the company, too.

The Taming of the Shrew was another of the O'Toole triumphs at Stratford. Again, however, Bernard Levin hedged his bets. 'Mr Peter O'Toole, when he stops barking, gives the impression that in another production he would make a fine, rough Petruchio. The wager scene at the end, when the tumult has died, comes off capitally, making the heart ache for what might have been.'

But Milton Shulman in the *Evening Standard,* had no such reservations. 'In Peter O'Toole,' he wrote, 'we have the most aggressive, virile dominating Petruchio in years. Any woman who stood in his way would be instantly blown apart by a puff or a sneeze. It is a marvellously comic performance which will put heart into even the most brow-beaten husband in the audience.'

His was such an important name now that whatever he did seemed to cause a stir. At the end of 1960, he had a walk-on part in a BBC TV play, *Song of the March Hare*. He came on at the beginning and at the end, didn't receive a penny for his trouble or get a line in the credits. But some actors complained vociferously to the BBC, claiming that O'Toole was helping put other less fortunate actors out of work. It was then pointed out that if O'Toole hadn't done it, an extra already employed in the play would have taken the part.

Why did he do it? He knew the producer—and it had become something of a fad among successful young performers to 'do a Hitchcock'.

And everyone did seem to be after Peter O'Toole. Now Elizabeth Taylor herself stepped in to try and waylay him for a new film idea—while *Cleopatra* continued to notch up more noughts in losses due to still further delays in starting work on filming.

She and her then husband, Eddie Fisher, decided that O'Toole would be the perfect co-star for the film she wanted to make of Tolstoy's *Anna Karenina*. 'We think that Peter is one of the finest actors in the whole world,' said Fisher. He had already gone backstage during the run of *The Taming of the Shrew* to tell him so. And if Eddie Fisher was not the world's greatest authority on Shakespeare, he and Miss Taylor had access to enough money to make that point somewhat irrelevant.

Peter drove to London and met the Fishers at the Dorchester. He won forty pounds from Elizabeth at blackjack. As far as she was concerned, *Anna Karenina* went the same way. It was never made. As things were to turn out, Peter had no cause to worry.

To Peter Hall, O'Toole was the bright star in the Stratford firmament. He was signed up for a long-term contract with the company. Hall knew they would be of great mutual benefit to each other, and big plans were being made for him. And then a name came up that changed everything—T. E. Lawrence.

Six

IN A WAY that was not easily explained, an actor who seemed most at home with Shakespeare had captured the headlines. People who had never seen a work by the Bard found the young actor fascinating. Those who can remember that far back said that the only thing comparable to Peter's effect on an audience was the way Al Jolson used to wow an audience in totally different shows on Broadway.

When Peter Hall announced that O'Toole was going to fly the Atlantic just to see a play in New York, it was hardly surprising that all the papers carried it as headlines in the biggest type available. The reason was that Hall wanted his new star to see the way an important new play starring Sir Laurence Olivier was being handled. It was another accolade for Peter.

Olivier had scored great critical acclaim for his title role in *Becket,* Jean Anouilh's play about the murder in Canterbury of Thomas à Becket. The play was about to be brought to London by the newly-renamed Royal Shakespeare Company, which had just taken over the lease of the Aldwych Theatre.

Hall knew that Peter would be perfect in the role of Henry II—Eric Porter would play Olivier's part—but he still wanted Peter to benefit from the performances of Sir Laurence and Anthony Quinn, who played the part he had earmarked for him. The £150 fare was an investment from which he knew he would reap big dividends.

It was a memorable weekend, as Peter Hall remembered.

'We were there for seventy-two hours,' he told me. 'It was Peter's first trip to New York and he was so excited, I don't think he went to sleep at all for that time. We stayed at the Algonquin and he just went from one place to the other, meeting people, talking.' It all seemed to bode well for a superb, memorable *Becket*.

And then came the mention of a film about Lawrence of Arabia.

Sam Spiegel had decided to make the film and was already thinking about two possible actors for the title role. Marlon Brando he was sure had the international pull that was required—he hadn't yet made *Mutiny On The Bounty,* a film for which Peter, too, had been tentatively offered a part. But Brando said no to *Lawrence.* It wasn't his sort of role.

Spiegel then went to Albert Finney, who was offered the film as part of a three-part contract. Finney decided he liked the freedom he had experienced in *Saturday Night And Sunday Morning* and declined, too. That was when Peter was approached—somewhat reluctantly, it turned out, since Spiegel had not exactly enjoyed Peter's first film test.

O'Toole seemed from the start to want the part. 'This is going to be one of the most important pictures ever made,' he said when the news reached the press. 'And it's not a part I am likely to turn down.'

It was, however, news to Peter Hall. Not only did he expect Peter to turn it down, he couldn't understand how he could possibly consider it. *Becket* was practically signed and sealed. His contract with the Shakespeare company was most certainly already signed. Under that agreement, O'Toole was allowed to undertake filming if it didn't interfere with his Stratford commitments. But *Lawrence of Arabia* wouldn't be one of those pictures at all. It would have to be shot on location and would take a great deal of time. He couldn't do both. The result was that both Peters stuck in their heels and the lawyers were called in.

It was to be the first of a whole series of legal hassles in Peter O'Toole's career. A couple of them would before long feature Mr Spiegel, too, although this was the only occasion when they were to be on the same side.

The announcement that the search for a Lawrence was at an end was made by Columbia Pictures, the corporation that would distribute the movie to be made by Spiegel's Horizon Films. Stratford received the news in what the gossip columns called stunned amazement. Peter Hall was furious, although he was playing it cool in statements intended for public consumption.

The trouble was over the business of time. Peter Hall said that his company would 'bend over backwards' to accommodate O'Toole so that his schedule could take in both the Shakespeare season and the Lawrence film. But it was clear that this was going to be impossible, and it was the company that had the contract that counted—not Mr Spiegel.

The film's director, David Lean, couldn't understand it either. It was Lean's presence that convinced Peter to sign up for the film. Not only would it be the greatest opportunity of his career to make a film of that importance, but the prestigious hand of Lean—who already had some very impressive work to his credit, ranging from *Blithe Spirit* and *Brief Encounter* to *Great Expectations* and the Oscar-winning *Bridge on the River Kwai*—meant that it was to be very big indeed. But Lean was not going to allow his plans to be interrupted either.

The *Lawrence* movie was to be shot in Jordan and work would begin in February 1961. They would be busy with the desert location shots for at least three months and probably four. Then there would be at least as much time needed on filming in London afterwards.

That plainly cut out Hall's *Becket* plans. Rehearsals for that were due to begin only a month after the cameras had started rolling in the desert, and the opening had been set for 25 April. The fact that the play would probably run for six to nine months was rapidly becoming immaterial.

Hall told me: 'I felt very badly let down and betrayed. And so did a great number of actors and actresses who were trying to make the RSC work. Perhaps we were naive in thinking that those sort of commitments matter. I think a number of actors felt let down, because an awful lot was riding on it. *Becket* was a package and Peter had been a very important part of it. Not having him in the play may have meant that we wouldn't have kept the rights to play it.'

One can understand how he felt. Here was the brightest new star seen in Britain in a generation—'I had no doubt at all he would one day be knighted'—appearing to sabotage one of the most ambitious schemes for the theatre yet launched in the country, at precisely the time the new Royal Shakespeare Company was coming into existence.

'We were opening at the Aldwych in the face of a great deal of opposition,' Sir Peter recalled. 'There was opposition from other West End theatre managers, from the critics, the Arts Council—who all thought we should stay at Stratford. Binkie Beaumont, of H.M.Tennents, ran a vigorous campaign to stop me getting a West End theatre. But we had done it—without a penny subsidy.

'It was a huge gamble. I was backed by the Stratford board and the Chairman, Sir Fordham Flower, to take the Aldwych for a season and try to show everybody that we merited some grant.'

One of Hall's principal weapons in trying to achieve that was the 'considerable coup' in getting the *Becket* play for his new theatre, particularly for what was intended as part of a repertory season. The deal had been struck between Hall himself and the playwright, Anouilh, and one of the most persuasive reasons for achieving it was the fact that O'Toole and Porter would be playing the lead roles.

'The blow was when Spiegel asked Peter to play Lawrence and he said yes. I told him that we had an agreement and he said words to the effect that, "I know we have an agreement but I'm going to do it."

'It was a very severe blow indeed because the whole enterprise might well have floundered. I am not naive enough to believe that you can hold an actor against his will. I knew how important Lawrence was to Peter. I also knew how important the start of the RSC was to us. He could have become a film star six months later.

'The lawyers were involved because had I lost the play—as I might have done—the whole season might have been in ruins, and so would the whole project of the RSC. We investigated all that because so much depended on it. We couldn't have made him go on the stage. Everyone must have his own morality.'

O'Toole himself was trying not to get involved. He said, it was up to his advisers. The advisers were pressing him not to give way. There was the inevitable talk of legal proceedings being taken. But Peter Hall realised the truth of what Jules Buck and the others on O'Toole's legal team were saying— contract or no contract, there was very little way of forcing an actor to go on stage—any stage—against his will. Particularly to give the kind of performance they had been depending on him to give.

Eventually the Royal Shakespeare Company admitted defeat. 'In the event it didn't matter,' Hall told me. 'We managed all right without him.' Christopher Plummer took over the role and the company stayed at the Aldwych for two decades. And Peter Seamus O'Toole began a totally new career less than two years after his initial success in *The Long And The Short And The Tall.*

He has since described the making of the Lawrence film as more of an experience than simply an acting job, and it is easy enough to see why. For the first time he was being treated to the trappings of superstardom: servants, the best accommodation, the finest food—although Peter was always much more concerned with the quality of the liquid than any more solid consumption. His salary was supposed to be £150,000 for three films, although it was never publicly disclosed. However, Peter did say afterwards that it was sufficient to buy a twenty-thousand-pound house in Heath Street, Hampstead.

But then he wasn't actually paid a salary at all. Sam Spiegel had engaged the services of Keep Films Ltd, who were playing a nice game of schizophrenia. They were making *Lawrence* at the same time as producing a movie called *Operation Snatch,* a comedy being filmed in Gibraltar, in which Peter—needless to say—was not appearing himself. And that was the way he wanted it. He saw himself as a combination of the actor-managers of old, and Ingmar Bergman who seemed to see nothing wrong in making a fortune and being an artistic success at the same time.

Among the actors in that film was James Villiers. For a time Peter was on hand, supervising production on behalf of Keep Films. He and Villiers would go for lunch most days. 'It was fun,' he recalled. 'But then at about four minutes to two, he would turn to me and say: "Right, Jim. Back to work." That was Peter the boss, rather than Peter the friend.'

He wasn't being remotely unpleasant, Villiers maintained, when he told me the story. 'There was no way that Peter could be unpleasant. But he was certainly playing the governor, rather than the mate.'

Nobody could doubt that *Lawrence of Arabia* was going to be a superb opportunity for him to spread wings which it seemed had only just started flexing themselves. It could also be a horrendous disaster, but reason dictated otherwise.

Peter had to agree to certain demands before a contract with Keep Films could be signed. First of all, he had to make two more films for Sam Spiegel. He also had to agree to dye his hair blond. That much was easy. The producer demanded one other thing—another nose job. It had to be just the way Lawrence had his, short, straight and very English.

Lawrence of Arabia is a magnificent story that was well enough known in outline to have become part of folklore— the British officer who dresses up as a Bedouin to lead an Arab revolt. That much every schoolboy and girl knows.

In 1960 when the project was first talked about, Alec

Guinness had had a notable stage success in a play called *Ross*—the name Lawrence took when he joined the RAF as an aircraftsman, his rank as a colonel and his Arabian adventures behind him.

But the detail of Lawrence's life—his astonishing capacity for upsetting authority, his megalomania, his sado-masochistic tendencies and, above all, in the more sheltered days at the beginning of that decade, his homosexuality, were unknown quantities. To most, he symbolised the strange but undeniable love felt by a number of Britons both for the desert and the Arabs who inhabited it. The story has, too, most of the classic ingredients of an 'Eastern'—a Western fought on the back of camels—with plenty of shooting and panoramas of a bleak landscape that is never less than beautiful. It is the stuff of bestselling fiction except that it is an historic document.

Peter was strongly marked by his two 'bosses' on the film. Particularly David Lean who came to Peter with the part after seeing him in *The Day They Robbed The Bank Of England*. 'The most important influence in my life has been David Lean,' Peter has said, 'I graduated in Lean, took my BA in Lean.'

And then there was Mr Spiegel, who could never quite forget the experience of that early film test. 'I was Spiegelised. No doubt about it. Stardom is insidious. It creeps through your toes. You don't realise what's happening until it reaches your nut. And that's when it becomes dangerous.'

The problem was that Mr Spiegel thought that Peter was fairly dangerous himself. 'Sam thought I was a tearaway,' he said soon after starting work on the movie. 'He thought I lived up a tree. He took a lot of convincing, I can tell you.'

The convincing began when they met at London's plush but sedate Connaught Hotel. As Peter took off his coat, a bottle of whisky fell to the floor. 'I can tell you, it was like the Arctic,' he said afterwards. The ice eventually began to melt—if only slightly.

Soon after that meeting, Spiegel rang Peter to offer him the part officially. 'Oh, yes,' said O'Toole pretending very effectively not to be impressed. 'Is it a speaking part?'

'Don't make such jokes,' said the producer.

Spiegel is nothing, however, if he is not a product of the film industry. He knows when to say the right things to the press. With Peter signed and ready to go, he was determined to make him out to be a gift of rain in the middle of a drought. 'O'Toole,' he declared, 'was probably the most heady blend of sensitivity and vitality I have known in an actor. He is one of those very rare specimens, and the contradictions in Lawrence's character make this O'Toole's greatest asset in the part.'

Spiegel had really wanted Finney for the part, and Peter sensed it from his first meeting with the producer. Before he became 'Spiegelised', he found it very difficult indeed to fit into the Hollywood scene. He was flown over to the movie capital by Spiegel to meet the Columbia executives—each of whom seemed to have bigger and plusher offices than the one he had seen before. Their cigars grew, too, in inverse proportion to the size of the man himself. One of them said to him, 'When I see you, I see six million dollars.' It was intended as a compliment. Peter did not see it that way. 'How would you like a punch up the throat?' O'Toole asked. The executive thought it was very funny and laughed till his cigar nearly choked him. Peter said he was quite serious—and so they got down to business.

And yet Peter was determined to enjoy every minute of it, an attitude somewhat different from that of Col T. E. Lawrence, although it is probable the soldier would have understood the actor as well as the actor quite obviously understood him. As Nat Brenner had suspected, there was certainly a feeling that Peter had the seeds of self-destruction about him, a condition that Lawrence would have understood well. They both lived dangerously, Lawrence in the desert, riding his motorcycle in the fatal crash with which the film began (it was, incidentally, filmed with Peter strapped to a trailer being pulled by the camera car); burning his fingers with matches—'of course, it hurts, the secret is not to mind'—and Peter with his succession of drinking parties and other escapades which worried the insurance companies tremendously.

He was like Lawrence in other ways, too. The sometimes filthy, generally untidy khaki-clad officer preened himself when awarded the pristine kuffia and white robes of an Arab chieftian, and Peter O'Toole, who had worn the shabby jerseys and threadbare corduroys as a RADA student, now enjoyed the luxury of being considered important, although clothes were rarely his principal consideration. But life was not all easy for him. He was suffering severe stomach pains and was advised to give up drinking. Peter saw no need to do so.

If he wasn't the obvious choice for Lawrence—and this really is the supreme compliment—it now seems inconceivable that Lawrence himself looked anything other than like Peter O'Toole. And yet he didn't. For one thing, O'Toole was at least eleven inches taller than the diminutive five foot five inches Lawrence stood—although some accounts say he was only five foot two inches, a fact that seemed to worry a number of Arabs whom O'Toole met who had known Lawrence. When one of them pointed this out, Peter pulled his dagger from the belt around his white robe and looked about to amputate the offending inches. The Arab almost collapsed with fright. It was another perfect O'Toole performance and helped lighten an atmosphere that was frequently tense.

It was all set to be an outstanding picture. David Lean directing. Peter O'Toole starring and with him Omar Sharif as Ali, the Bedouin whom he meets after a shooting incident and who becomes his bosom buddy. There was Jack Hawkins as General Alenby, Donald Wolfit as another general, Anthony Quayle as the British officer who finds Lawrence very difficult to understand and Alec Guinness now switching roles and playing the Emir Faisal.

No one could say it was an easy movie to put together.

Three thousand extras had to be moved across the Jordan desert and fed and watered, using aerial methods never dreamed of in Lawrence's day. And some of them had to be women—which was difficult because no Moslem woman would allow her face to be exposed on the screen. In the end, several hundred Christian females had to be imported from Egypt—and earned more in the course of a couple of weeks than they had in their lives before. There were no women with speaking roles in the picture.

Peter had to involve himself in Middle East politics during his time in Jordan. He was advised to discontinue the practice he had adopted in the past year of wearing a Star of David round his neck. It was a talisman his mother had given him as an appropriate jewel for a successful Shylock. Now he was told that it could bring him all sorts of things in Jordan, but good luck was unlikely to be one of them. However, he kept a few options open as far as superstitions were concerned. If he couldn't wear a charm that might be considered pro-Israeli in a country officially at war, Irish nationalism presented no problems at all. Consequently, he now supplemented his green socks with a green jacket. It went everywhere with him, even in the heat of an African summer. Peter and Omar Sharif—he called him 'Cairo Fred'—became close friends on the set, each admiring the other's capacity for enjoying himself.

Peter arrived in Jordan three months before filming began, reading and re-reading Lawrence's *Seven Pillars of Wisdom*—which he thought was a terrible book—and everything else ever printed about him. He also spent time absorbing the nation's folklore as well as its history and geography.

The filming of *Lawrence* actually took two years and three months. As Peter said at the time, it was two years, three months of actually being T. E. Lawrence.

From Jordan, the team moved on to Spain, where they all tried to join in the high life as much as possible—although Peter was to describe it as being 'like Pontefract with sunshine'. Among the people he met was a young model named

April Ashley. He found her deliciously feminine—soft, creamy skin, gently curving hips and breasts that would have delighted readers of *Playboy*. April, formerly a sailor, was the most celebrated transsexual of the day. She and Peter had met before when he was at Bristol, but it was not until now that they became friendly. She didn't recognise him at first; the hair and the nose made all the difference that Sam Spiegel had wanted.

'One of the most sensitive men I have ever met,' she told me. 'Devastatingly attractive and intelligent.' It was his intellect that attracted her most, she said. 'Even when playing the hell-raiser, he would open his mouth and speak with a command of the language Shakespeare would have admired. It is just incredible to listen to him talk.'

Their first meeting in the midst of the *Lawrence* filming was at a party in Marbella where April and her then husband had a home.

She became so friendly with Peter and Omar that the three of them would go off for, she says, three- and four-day—or rather night-time drinking binges. 'Peter never seemed to eat a thing, but every now and again he'd say to Omar, "I'm just going off to feed April".' After drinking at a succession of local bars, they would end up at a nightclub, literally dancing and drinking the night away. Sharif was a good friend to Peter at the time; staying with him sometimes until he drank himself to insensibility, not leaving his side in case something serious happened.

Alcohol by now had become more than just a means of enjoying himself. As another friend with him at the time told me, Peter was discovering that if he got through three bottles of Burgundy, he could fall asleep. Without it, he would be lucky to nod off for more than an hour. Chronic insomnia was beginning to take its toll. And yet, as April said, 'The most astonishing thing about Peter was his sensitivity. Even when he was drunk, he would know exactly what was going on. Even when he'd been out all night, he'd be on the set next morning, line perfect.'

The celebrities courted them. King Saud of Saudi Arabia

was there at the time and invited Peter for dinner. 'The hell with that,' he said, 'I've just spent six months with his lot in the desert. I'm going off to get drunk.'

Peter's parents came to see him at work in Spain. Patty couldn't resist the opportunity of going to see a bullfight while he was there and insisted that Peter go with him. Now that was asking too much. Peter who would all but swoon at the sight of the tomato ketchup used in the battle scenes of Lawrence, was likely to do much more faced with the real thing oozing from the skins of wounded bulls. So April was asked to accompany the 'Captain' on his visit to the one 'sporting' event where he wouldn't be expected to take any bets.

Halfway through the spectacle, April told me she had a feeling something was happening in the bar. It was. From outside the building could be heard the sound of thumps, shouts and punches, and above it all the voice of Peter Seamus O'Toole who had fired the whole event by standing a series of particularly potent drinks to the entire assembly, egging everyone on.

It was a fun day. And there were plenty more like them. 'I don't think for a minute there was any inner reason for his drinking like that,' says April. 'Certainly, he wasn't unhappy. He talked about Sian all the time—how much he adored and worshipped her. I think he just loved to drink.'

But it was easy to see that the drink made him maudlin—such as the night when April made a spectacular entrance at the opening of a new bodega in Jerez de la Frontera run by the Marques de Domecq d'Usquain. Peter was on one arm, Omar Sharif on the other. The Spanish royal family were guests of honour, but it was the O'Toole party that had the flashbulbs popping.

During the evening, a friend approached April. 'I think you ought to go over to Peter. He's sitting at the bar, crying.'

She rushed to the side of a now positively howling Peter O'Toole. 'What's the matter?' she asked him, almost weeping now herself. 'What's happened to you?'

81

He found it difficult to come out with the answer between sobs. 'I really can't believe it,' he told her. 'It's about you.'

'Me?' asked April.

'Yes,' he replied, 'You. At least six people have been up to me in the past half hour, telling me about your background. I really can't understand how people can be so cruel. It must be hell for you.'

'Oh, darling, don't worry about it,' she said.

But the mood carried on. Later that night he was not only totally drunk, but fighting drunk, punching and being punched by almost anyone who said the slightest thing with which he may have disagreed. When someone made a remark about April, both Peter and Omar swung out.

She took Peter back to the Swan Hotel where both he and Omar were staying. Getting undressed soon afterwards, she heard Peter's door slam and footsteps clattering to the nearest elevator. O'Toole was going back to the bar. She decided to keep him away from drink—and from getting his already somewhat pummelled face even more damaged—by inveigling him back to her bedroom.

Their relationship, she stresses, was strictly platonic. But they did sleep together. 'Peter enjoys a cuddle as much as anyone else.' Next day when there was conveniently no filming—she had to promise not to open the curtains lest he suffer the effects of daylight.

'He had this marvellous colour in his face and hands and arms. But when he stripped off, he was like an El Greco. The rest of him looked green.'

Omar Sharif was dark brown all over, however. One night, April left Peter for Sharif's bed, where they did make love. She told him of her sex change operation while they were in bed together. Later she crept back to Peter's room. 'Traitor,' said O'Toole and both of them then fell asleep laughing.

Sian knew what he had been up to, April says. 'But she was never worried. Nor was there any reason for her to be.'

Plainly, April and Peter got on very well and she knew a great deal about him. 'I always felt,' she told me, 'that he had

82

a dislike of homosexuals, although he was always very kind to them.'

He was certainly kind to her. April told him she wanted to be an actress. 'Don't,' he warned forcibly. 'Don't, darling, those bastards would never let you alone.' He was, she said, absolutely right.

When filming finished in Spain, the company moved on to Africa for more of what might have been considered the right ambiance. They chose a part of Morocco much admired by film makers—in wintertime. They made a mistake of going there in July and August, a time of year when the place resembled nothing less than an open-air incubator.

It was so hot there, in fact, that while they were filming, the French Foreign Legion were using the area as a punishment centre for wrongdoers, a sort of Devil's Island without sea-water surrounding it. This was particularly tough on Peter, who is one of Nature's lovers of the Great Indoors. His idea of heaven, he has said often enough, is a smoke-filled room.

Lawrence would not only have tolerated it, but made it seem as though he, of course, enjoyed every penitential soul-cleansing moment of it. This was another way in which he and the hero of the picture were diametrically opposed. O'Toole didn't even believe in suffering for the sake of charity. 'The best thing to do,' he said once, 'is to keep your cake shut and send a few bob. That St Francis of Assisi bit of whipping off your knickers and joining a leper colony doesn't work for most people.'

Certainly, he saw no reason to suffer while learning to ride a camel. Lawrence may have done it in a day, so Peter O'Toole had to know how it felt to learn that quickly. But, he reasoned, he didn't have to suffer quite as much when it came down to the bottom of things. He had one moment on the camel's back and decided he had had enough. He found some foam rubber, cut it to shape and thereafter found riding on the humped beasts not quite such an excruciating experience. The Arabs around him stared incredulously. At first, it seemed as though they regarded it as nothing short of sacrilege. So he felt honour-bound to explain: 'You can all be good Bedouins, stones of the desert, but this is a very delicate Irish ass.'

He described that event as 'one of the most important contributions ever made to Arab culture'.

Nothing is as infectious as envy. Before long, one Arab, then another and finally all the extras riding with him asked for similar aids to rear comfort. Hundreds of yards of foam rubber were imported from London at Peter's request.

He told writer Tim Satchell that it was the hardest bit of stuntman activity he ever practised—riding round three thousand miles of desert without brakes. All he could hope for was that when he hit the beast on the side of the head, it would start moving in a series of ever-decreasing circles.

Camel bites left two of his fingers out of action for months, and these were not the only injuries. He sprained both ankles, suffered agonising pain from sunburned feet, cracked one ankle bone, dislocated his spine, strained a ligament and fell on his head sufficiently heavily to be knocked unconscious on two different occasions.

Almost everyone working on the film with him thought that Peter coped as well with the people as he had with the camels. He was no less warm with a teaboy than he was with King Hussein—and seemingly no less awed by the King than he was by the teaboy. And he was not beyond offering advice—even to Hussein. When he and the King got together, Peter asked the then young monarch—he is about three years younger than the actor—about the country's economy. The King was proud of his nation, but, despite his own fleet of cars and aeroplanes, had to admit that it was poor. 'I have the perfect solution,' said Peter. 'Bottle the Jordan.'

If only the film could have been 'bottled' by then. But even when the crew moved back to England, it wasn't all over. There was, for one thing, the first shot to be filmed—of Lawrence crashing to his death on the motorcycle. It could have been the end of Peter's career—and his life. Just as the scene was being filmed, the metal bar connecting the trailer with the camera-car snapped. It had been tested a dozen times, and yet metal fatigue was diagnosed. The only thing that stopped Peter being catapulted into the road was a fairly flimsy piece of rope.

He said at the time: 'Afterwards, we all climbed in the back of the car with Lean. No one said a word. We all sat there in silence, smoking, looking at the floor. But I think it was only Lawrence up there, teasing.'

Had that happened earlier in the filming, Sam Spiegel might have thought it somewhat more than a mere tease— and from a power greater than the spirit of T. E. Lawrence. The film was virtually uninsurable—and with Peter in almost every single scene, the producer would have liked to have kept him in a satin-lined, air-conditioned coffin between takes. He was not allowed to fly, or to drive. 'Sam,' said Peter at the time, 'treats me more like Rin Tin Tin than a working actor.'

Considering his investment—1961 estimates of the budget hovered around the three million dollars mark; a huge sum for the time—it was perhaps hardly surprising.

Peter wondered sometimes about the economic factors in making a film. Not only did *Lawrence* take more than two years of his time, he had to get used to waiting two weeks between shots. One particular scene took a lot longer.

David Lean decided when they got back to London that a close-up was necessary. It was shot exactly two years after the rest of the scene had been photographed. So, in the space of a couple of minutes, a twenty-nine-year-old Peter O'Toole is seen virtually simultaneously with a thirty-one-year-old version of the same man.

The work was done in a tiny room in Hammersmith—as Peter has described it, 'with an old blue wall and a bit of dry ice'. The director issued instructions one minute and consulted the moviola on which the original scenes had been shot the next, editing and filming simultaneously.

It was the scene when Omar Sharif galloped towards

85

O'Toole from the mirage in the film's opening scene. The director felt he needed another close-up of Peter's reactions at that moment. As Peter said, the results were there for all to see—filmed 'in our little armpit in Hammersmith'.

'Eight goddam seconds and two years of my life had gone from me!'

It was, however, par for the course for O'Toole at this time. 'Lawrence,' he said, 'I was obsessed by the man. And it was bad. A true artist should be able to jump into a bucket of crap and come out smelling of violets. But I spent two years and three months thinking about nothing but Lawrence. Day after day. It was bad for me. It killed my acting later on.' There are others who will agree with that, and some who say it merely helped hone a promising career into fulfilment.

Peter bases his judgment on the fact that *Lawrence* is practically the only film of his he has watched—and then only about forty minutes of it on television. 'I thought, "Who is that pudding, that poor, coy twit with the twinkling blue eyes? My God, it's me!" I could not watch more because my mind wandered.'

On another occasion, he said: 'Oh, it's painful seeing it all there on a screen—solidified, embalmed. Once a thing is solidified, it stops being a living thing. That's why I love the theatre. It's the art of movement.'

When filming ended, he wound up in hospital to be treated for all the assembled injuries resulting from the production—to say nothing of exhaustion. He had lost two stone in weight in the process of 'digging deep inside myself to find the right chemistry for this gent called Lawrence'. As he said, he 'dug a lot of Peter O'Toole as well'.

As soon as he could, he tried to do a variety of different things—including a one-night-stand reading from Sean O'Casey's autobiography, *Pictures In The Hallway*, at London's Mermaid Theatre. That was digging, too.

What he thought he had unearthed was the knowledge that riches and success would not spoil him. Did he want a Cadillac, a press agent (then seemingly the ultimate status symbol), a swimming pool and a supply of blondes ready to feed his every whim? 'Hell, no,' he said at the time, 'I'll be back to Connemara in the morning.'

He didn't adore the trappings of stardom, and it was fair to surmise he would be happier with a glass of Scotch in a crowded public bar than sipping champagne at an elegant Hollywood party. He was never happier than when drinking with old RADA mates like Albert Finney and Alan Bates. 'People think we're scruffy—and they're dead right,' he said. 'The scruffs, the slags. It's a pretty hard school. You wouldn't last three minutes if you didn't have your wits about you.'

It sometimes looked, however, as though it were more a style for style's sake, a feeling that it identified him with a group of Peter Pans and therefore he couldn't grow old and respectable. It also occasionally looked like inverse snobbery, as though he were frightened of people thinking he had renounced his 'criminal class' roots. He went out of his way to show that success had not spoiled him. But this did not mean he was not going to enjoy the riches that were now his.

He did go to Ireland when he left hospital, and to several of his other old haunts. When in Bristol, he ended up spending a night in the police station cells. He had a tussle with a bollard while under the influence, and lost his driving licence.

Peter gave vent to iconoclastic impulses whenever possible. Soon after all the location work on Lawrence had been completed, he was invited to be guest of honour and judge at a fancy dress ball, the theme being, 'The Mysterious East'. How he could have agreed to attend defies imagination, unless it was simply the prospect of readily available booze, but agree he did and got more and more bored as the evening wore on. In fact, his boredom developed into a serious antagonism towards the very region being honoured by the ball. He had quite simply had enough of people dressing up as Arabs.

They were marched before him: elegant men who could have played Lawrence themselves; fat short men in red tarbooshes who might have spent the earlier part of the day in a bazaar; busty women undressed as belly dancers. Finally, he spotted the winner—a man whose Eastern ancestry might have gone back to Whitechapel but no further. He was dressed up as a bag of sugar. That was what Peter called courage—and he decided to reward it. Second prize went to another rebel—dressed up as Guy Fawkes. The organisers were singularly unamused.

If being a success was submitting to the need to celebrate that achievement, then he was prepared to go along with it. Certainly, he loved the money that being a film star gave him. He once told a writer: 'In the early days, in the greedy, skint, ambitious days, I would have done anything, practically anything, to get on. Money and success, I grabbed at it. I was such a greedy little grabber.'

But that was nothing compared to the 'greed' with which he ate up the months waiting for *Lawrence* to open, and that waiting made him yearn to be back in the live theatre. He once said: 'The theatre is the art of the moment. I'm in love with ephemera and I hate permanence.' Neither did he like very much the way people were already saying he was being ruined by success. 'Let's face it,' he said. 'More people have been butchered and ruined by failure.' He had already done his bit to make sure that *Lawrence of Arabia,* at least, would be no failure.

Spiegel, showman to the last, decided to leave the cinema-going public with the distinct impression that he and he alone had been responsible for the great discovery they were facing in *Lawrence of Arabia.* Ignoring the success of *The Day They Robbed The Bank Of England* and leaving aside totally the impact Peter had already made on an almost worshipping theatre public, the opening credit announced that the film was 'Introducing Peter O'Toole'.

It was an introduction the audience was happy to make. As though lining up to shake his hand personally, they swarmed to box offices throughout the world to see a film that in 1963 not only had the critics excitedly welcoming O'Toole's performance but which, as one might expect, was sold with all the ballyhoo and advertising Columbia could find. It was a 'roadshow' film that ran in theatres from Alaska to Australia—and practically every other country in the world in between—for months on end.

It got off to a fine start with a London premiere attended by the Queen. The *Sunday Express* described it as 'magnificent' and speculated what Peter's next role would be. They had no doubt it would be in the next big blockbuster about to go before the cameras, *My Fair Lady,* in which Peter would play Professor Higgins. His name came up in various Warner Brothers discussions but Jack Warner, the head of the studio, had come to the conclusion that it would be safer to go with Rex Harrison, who had already made the part his own both on Broadway and at London's Drury Lane.

Proof that his performance had got the industry talking was when he was nominated for an Academy Award. In the end it was won by Gregory Peck for his magnificent work in *To Kill A Mockingbird.* Another hot-tipped favourite had been Jack Lemmon in *Days Of Wine And Roses.* Peter has been told that he will never win an Oscar until he settles down and lives in Hollywood. And it has happened five more times. Always the blushing bridesmaid. Never to date the bride.

If there were complaints, it was in the way exhibitors treated it. In 1970, one could almost feel the tears in the ink when the *New York Times* sadly reported 'Look what they've done to Lawrence of Arabia now'.

Fifteen minutes 'absolutely crucial to the plot, characterisations and dramatic rhythm of the film have been removed', complained Stephen Farber and readers went on sharing his grumbles in the correspondence columns for weeks.

In fact, the film was now thirty-five minutes shorter than it had been during the start of its initial run. In the course of that showing, twenty perhaps not so crucial minutes had already been snipped.

Now, not only were some of the most important illustrations of Lawrence's megalomania removed, but even the vital scene near the end when a medical officer slaps his face and calls him a 'filthy little wog'.

But, Oscar or no Oscar, no one would disagree with Farber when he said: 'Its appeal was universal. But maybe because we did not know much about T. E. Lawrence before seeing the film, we did not come to it with the preconceptions that kept many older people from appreciating its richness. We saw the film fresh and it mattered. *Lawrence of Arabia* was one of the new films made during the sixties that touched the imaginations of a generation.'

And Peter himself said that it wasn't so much a film, it was an experience—'only the film got in the way of the experience'.

Seven

LAWRENCE OF ARABIA made a new man of Peter O'Toole—at least in the public's mind. And that was the problem. It created a monster out of a triumph.

On the one hand, it is a film of which he has always been proud. On the other, it is a yardstick by which everything else, twenty years later, is still judged; a sort of *Citizen Kane*, although luckier than that one was for Orson Welles for Peter has found ways of getting close to his achievement since.

Lawrence was both a foretaste of good things to come and a reason for regret every time he widely missed the target. It represented success, brilliance, and a feeling among audiences that they were being cheated if the steely O'Toole eyes weren't mesmerising them in a slightly crazed Lawrence pose every time they saw him on the screen.

He was now totally hooked on one incontrovertible fact—he was a film superstar, open to offers—once his contractual obligations to Mr Spiegel were satisfied—that seemed to be spelled out in telephone numbers. He didn't, however, want that to be his only life. It was as if *Lawrence* launched him on two totally different trajectories: the career he wanted as an actor and the one he found he couldn't do without, as a money-making machine. *Lawrence* was the film that gave millions, who would never have the possibility of seeing him on a stage, an opportunity to experience his brilliant acting achievement. There would, in the years to come, be other similar chances.

Money certainly was a powerful element, although he said afterwards: 'I never really enjoyed the blue-eyed, blond-haired nonsense I went in for after *Lawrence*. The romantic twits, the tormented bloody youths. I found them such a bore. But I did them professionally and to the best of my ability because they meant a steady income.'

And he changed the way he lived in order to fit the image the moguls wanted for him. The press told stories about his roustabout behaviour. The studios wanted him to seem the clean-cut, pristine-living film star forged in the image of Cary Grant.

'I never really cared how I looked,' he has said. 'It was the other people—they cared. So I had to care because if I looked untidy, it was an obstacle to making money.'

In truth, he didn't always look the way the moguls would have wished. And he didn't satisfy their requirements for gentlemanly behaviour, either. One writer once said that *Lawrence* provided him with a mantle that was too heavy for him to carry—so he became a wild uncontrollable hedonist. That was hardly true. If anything, the way he reacted to *Lawrence* was a tribute to himself and the way he saw the world. Success was not going to change him or spoil him. He was spoilt already. The man dubbed Old Iron Guts by others in the business would have been like that had he still been earning forty-five pounds a week in rep in Bristol.

Nor, he now liked to boast, was he rich. Every penny he owned and had made from *Lawrence* had gone into the house on Hampstead Heath. 'I'm skint,' he told *Daily Express* writer Peter Evans, who interviewed him at his home, and noted a baby's bonnet impaled on a piece of O'Toole-owned statuery. Kate's bonnet could have been owned by the child of a beggar, yet the bust on which it had been so unceremoniously draped had been sculpted by Jacob Epstein.

If he was without funds, it wasn't a strange situation for him. 'The only difference now,' he told Evans, 'is that I am luxuriously broke.' But he had no intention of changing his ways. 'Hell, if I started being cautious now, Sian would just put Kate under one arm and hop it.' But there were times when it seemed that a little caution would not have gone amiss.

The amazing thing is that this incredibly intelligent and articulate actor finds it very difficult indeed talking to a TV camera. Not that he let it worry him when he was the guest on BBC television's popular satyrical show *That Was The Week That Was*—he upset a number of people by appearing to ramble on about religion and politics. He then tried to give his impersonations of a whole succession of people—ranging from Moses to General de Gaulle—and throwing in an O'Toole impression of God for good measure.

In fact, Peter seemed to worry about very little—and with good cause. One newspaper reported him saying, 'I can't get over my good luck.' And good luck was something he had a-plenty. Sian and he appeared to have an idyllic marriage and loved baby Kate to distraction. One day when she fell over, she ran to Peter with a shattered pair of spectacles. 'Daddy,' she called, 'I've broken my eyes.' 'Don't worry, Kate,' he told her, soothingly. 'We'll get some more.' Both Sian and he worried together over an eye condition which rendered Kate nearly blind. But as the years wore on, the condition miraculously improved. And he would have been justified in thinking that his career would get better and better. There were certainly a number of opportunities ahead of him to make it so.

One of them was that at last he was going to play Henry II in *Becket*—although there was no satisfaction for Peter Hall in the fact. This time the role would be performed on screen with Richard Burton playing the Archbishop of Canterbury. He and O'Toole got on marvellously, sharing each other's taste for quality roles—as well as good liquor.

The film was produced by Hal Wallis, a veteran Hollywood man who for years had run the Warner Brothers studios. He had even been there when the first talkie, *The Jazz Singer*, starring Al Jolson, had been made. *Casablanca* and *Little*

Caesar were among the rosta of Wallis productions. 'I just knew that O'Toole would be brilliant,' he told me. 'I was not disappointed . . . I rang Sam Spiegel to ask him if he could let me see some footage on *Lawrence*. When I saw it, I knew that Peter was the man I wanted.'

Wallis then rang Peter to offer him the role. 'Who's playing Becket?' he asked.

'Richard Burton,' said Wallis.

'Marvellous,' said O'Toole.

He then rang Burton.

'Who's playing the King?' Burton asked.

'Peter O'Toole,' said the producer.

'Marvellous,' replied Burton.

When one actor admires another, it is a thing of beauty. There was no doubt about the way Burton regarded his colleague. Early on in the shooting, in 1964, he told the director, Peter Glenville: 'He's a marvellous bag of bones. Look after him.'

As usual, Peter ransacked the libraries, searching for everything he could find that would explain the complicated figure of Henry. He not only wanted to play him well, but to play him differently—as different from Lawrence as he could possibly make him. They were infinitely different characters, except that both did seem to have a masochistic streak. The look on Henry's face after being physically beaten at the end of the film did seem to bear an uncanny resemblance to that of Lawrence after suffering at the hands of the homosexual Turkish officer.

It is not easy, particularly for an actor of O'Toole's quality, to know exactly how he is going to interpret a part. Having read all he could about the historical aspect of Henry's life, he now wanted to find something in his personality on which he could latch; a detail that would prove the linchpin of his characterisation. He found it in a contemporary description of the monarch. Henry, it said, had a voice that sounded like a man's heel being rubbed against glass. A heel rubbed against glass? What could that possibly mean? So he tried it to find out. It was a deep resonant sound. The nearest comparison he could make, he decided, was with the voice of the bass, Paul Robeson.

It wasn't enough for him to think that. Now he had to prove it to himself. He bought a copy of every Robeson record he could find in the shops and played them for an hour each morning, attempting to sing over the voice, as though Robeson himself were going to be dubbing songs for him. This is the technique used by non-singing actors who have to be able to match every single mouth and tongue movement that on screen will appear to spring from their own larynxes.

When he went before the cameras the O'Toole voice, at least an octave lower than usual, sounded different enough. It was sufficient to lay the ghost of T. E. Lawrence—although few critics allowed themselves to forget the earlier role in their reviews. Not that it mattered. One critic described the picture as 'handsome, respectable—and boring'. However, it won him his second Oscar nomination in two years which wasn't bad—even if he didn't win.

Hal Wallis's hunch had worked. He knew that Peter would take to the story like a student determined to pass an exam. In one scene, when he said of Becket, 'will no one rid me of this meddlesome priest?'—Peter had to be drunk. He prepared himself for this the only way he knew how, by drinking—very heavily indeed.

The only problem was that union regulations demanded that filming end at 6 p.m. The mood had to be recreated the following morning. 'It was remarkable,' recalled Wallis. 'At 9.30 he had built himself up to the same state again.'

To show his gratitude, the producer told me he bought Peter two paintings by the Irish artist Jack Yeats, brother of W. B. Yeats. 'He was like a child getting a new toy,' Wallis said. There was another new toy at the time, too. It was while making the film that he acquired his first Rolls Royce.

One of the reasons for the success of the production was O'Toole's strong sense of cameraderie with Richard Burton—who has claimed that he was offered the role of the King first, but turned it down at the suggestion of Elizabeth Taylor who said that after being King Arthur in *Camelot,* and *Henry V* in the Shakespeare play, there were too many similarities in the roles. O'Toole simply says that Burton is a rogue working under an alias—his real name is Jenkins.

The endless hours spent waiting for their turn to go on the soundstage, or just parading in their ornate costumes, gave them ample opportunity to talk shop. They got round to discussing *Hamlet.* It was a play they both ought to do again before it was too late, said Burton. O'Toole agreed. Burton said he knew who he wanted as his director, Sir John Gielgud. Peter said he'd rather have Olivier. 'Let's toss for it,' he said, 'and see who wins.' Peter won, which is fortunate since he had already had an approach from Sir Laurence who was about to become director of the new National Theatre—due to open late in 1963 at the Old Vic in London's Waterloo Road—the same playhouse where Nat Brenner had spotted the O'Toole talent all those years before. Olivier wanted Peter to star in his first production there. Burton rightly decided that both of them couldn't play the part in London at more or less the same time and persuaded Gielgud to direct him in it in America.

For Olivier to have approached Peter was compliment enough. But the offer was more than just flattering, particularly since his film of the Prince of Denmark fourteen years earlier had established Olivier as the most brilliant Hamlet of modern times. Now he was offering Peter the chance to step into his shoes—under his own direction. Peter said yes immediately. The plan was to produce the play for an October 1963 opening. And it was to be a star-studded occasion.

But before starting work on *Hamlet,* Peter was to star in Bertolt Brecht's play, *Baal,* a project that seemed in no way likely to overlap the National date. It opened at the Phoenix Theatre in March 1963.

Baal is the story of a drunken, womanising, destitute old cabaret singer-poet who sees the degradation around him and has neither the will nor the courage to do anything about it. He leaves his mistress when she is pregnant, murders his only friend and shows too much attention to children, for wholly unpleasant reasons. It was the sort of role a number of producers had been trying to persuade Peter to play since his image as the wild man of the theatre had first been splattered around the gossip columns.

Baal was too esoteric to be obviously good box office. On the other hand, its sex scenes were franker than almost any yet seen in Britain. Girls in the cast wore so few clothes that extra heating had to be provided on stage. 'I think we will all get arrested,' Peter told *Scene* magazine. 'It makes Jimmy Porter and *The Ginger Man* seem like "Mrs Dale's Diary".'

His prognosis was not wrong. It was Brecht's first play and some say his worst, although eighteen years later it would be given a highly popular new lease of life in a television production starring pop singer David Bowie. It also arrived in London more than forty years after it had been written. But more crucial was the fact that Peter was physically and mentally exhausted and only realised it when on a live stage again. Even his voice didn't carry strongly enough. All that time riding camels and wiping the sand from his eyes had made him feel something like a bottle of Scotch diluted with at least three parts water.

Most of the critics didn't notice. But Herbert Kretzmer didn't like it at all. He listed the play as being among the most notable experiences during his hundred first nights writing for the paper. But that didn't mean to say it was one of the good ones. 'O'Toole . . . is supposed to be a disreputably ugly rake who captivates women by the sheer power of the life force within him,' he wrote. 'In fact, O'Toole never looks any more disreputable than Van Johnson with a five o'clock shadow, and his whole performance is contemptuous . . . agonisingly self-congratulatory.' Like his criticism of some of the work of Richard Harris and director Lindsay Anderson, the play was 'human waste . . . of some of the best actors walking the earth today'.

Other writers were a little kinder about Peter's return to the West End in *Baal*. 'Indifferently performed,' said *The Times*, 'his part would be both ludicrous and boring. But in this production Peter O'Toole delivers the lines with a harsh measured dignity that can make bombast sound like a passage from the Old Testament; and he plays with a fiery depravity that raises the character to Dostoyevskian grandeur.'

Milton Shulman took up the theme in the *Evening Standard*. 'It was all a bit like a strip cartoon,' he said. 'O'Toole cements these fragmentary situations into a cohesive whole through the sheer force of his personality. Whether he is seducing women, blinded with drink, crying to the stars or dying in misery, there is a blazing determination in his eyes and voice that still makes him a symbol of man's dignity in spite of the filth of both his body and his mind.'

Afterwards, Peter reflected that 'it wasn't the greatest success in the world. But it was good for the theatre.'

'I'm in love with ephemera and I hate permanence,' he once said. 'Acting is making words into flesh and I love classical acting because you need the vocal range of an opera singer, the movement of a ballet dancer. You have to be able to act. It's turning your whole body into a musical instrument on which you yourself play. It's more than behaviourism which is what you get in the movies. Christ! What are movies anyway? Just fucking moving photographs. But the theatre! There you have the impermanence that I love. It's a reflection of life somehow. It's . . . it's like building a statue of snow.'

He was at an age when he wanted to expand. Acting didn't have to be confined to the stage or the screen—big or small—in the conventional sense. When he was asked to honour Britain's veteran actress, Dame Sybil Thorndike, at a concert at the Royal Festival Hall, he accepted warmly. Giving praise to an older practitioner of his craft has always been one of his most endearing characteristics. For this occasion, he read from the diaries of the composer, Haydn, in a one-man show entitled *My Pleasures In London.*

The problem that faced him, however, was that Olivier's *Hamlet* at the National seemed to owe a great deal to the movies and to borrow too liberally from Shakespeare at the same time. Instead of the cut version which Sir Laurence had himself used in the film and with which Peter had scored his huge triumph at Bristol, the Old Vic audience heard every word Shakespeare wrote and saw every direction he included in the second quarto edition. The play lasted five hours fifteen minutes.

The disappointing result was that the man who had been described as the best stage Hamlet of the twentieth century was now in danger of being described as the worst.

He has said that Olivier 'turned me to stone' a couple of times as he gazed in his direction during rehearsals, but after the final rehearsal he addressed the cast with words that no actor will ever forget. 'Ladies and gentlemen,' he said emotionally—and modestly—'for the first time in living memory we have seen the real Hamlet.' Other people were not so sure.

Peter Hall who showed no animosity by going along to the first night—'I was terribly amused to note that the National couldn't get Peter for more than six weeks'—said that the difference between the two interpretations was immense. 'He wasn't the Hamlet he was. I have always admired him very much. I remember thinking that first time that he was a star. And what is your definition of a star? Someone you can't take your eyes off.'

One of the problems with this new version of the play was that there were so many distractions it was difficult to keep your eyes *on* him. But Peter's performance was anything but the brilliant tour-de-force people had been expecting.

Part of the fault may have been the way he regarded Shakespeare from the start. His respect for the Bard was obvious in the way he has always craved to play him. But he saw him differently from most actors. 'Shakespeare, for Christ's sake, (is) not a diety. His people . . . piss against the wall.'

He didn't do that exactly as Hamlet, but the people who turned up for the first night at the Old Vic were expecting something spectacular. So spectacular, in fact, that it was one of those evenings when the personalities in the audience rivalled those behind the curtain on stage, although Sir Laurence deliberately didn't want it to be more than a theatre occasion. No members of the Royal Family were present. Those who were there were mostly members of the profession—ranging from Leslie Caron to Shirley Bassey.

Before the company took up their positions in the wings, Sir Laurence pulled Peter on the sleeve. 'Are you ready?' he asked.

'For what?' asked O'Toole.

'For them. They're out there with their machine guns. It's your turn, son.'

As things were to turn out, the guns were in the hands of the critics. Peter knew that they would be and it was not a pleasant thought as he anticipated his first entrance. The energy he had for so long depended upon had gone. As he once told British journalist John Walker: 'I realised I'd lost. It was awful. Awful.'

If the critics were getting the big guns ready, the audience was there determined to show all the affection and sympathy that an actor can demonstrate to another member of his profession. Lady Redgrave—who not only had her husband, Sir Michael, in the cast as the King, but her daughter, Lynn, making her stage debut in a walk-on role—declared it to be 'the greatest night in the history of the theatre'. Even Vanessa—in the days before she dedicated herself to the workers—put on a gold dress to be there. If Olivier had asked Peter to put on a gold dress as Hamlet, he would probably have done that, too. He says now that he was much too influenced by Olivier 'far too influenced. I mean, really in-awe department'.

Being directed by a man who has played the part himself ought to be reason enough for danger signals to flash. Some directors could deliberately undercut their actors rather than risk allowing their own performances to pale in the shadow of something new. But nobody would suggest that Sir Laurence did that. But he did have a stylised view of the Prince based on the way he himself had interpreted him. And because of who he was, it was difficult—once having been flattered into accepting the role—not to follow the Olivier line.

Gone with the abbreviated Bristol version were the Hamlet whiskers. 'I conned myself,' said O'Toole seven years later. 'Larry beguiled me into every bloody trick—blond wigs, short shirts and . . . five and three-quarter hours on stage.' And then he added tellingly: 'Of course, I think it's the worst bloody play ever written. Actors do it out of vanity.'

Having admitted to that vanity, Peter had to take the consequences.

There were also problems with many of the innovations introduced to the play by Sean Kenny. The graveyard scene, for instance, was beset with problems. The grave opened electrically—which meant that on more than one occasion, it didn't open at all. When it did, there was a distinct risk of anyone nearby being fatally swallowed up by the machinery. Frank Finlay, one of the gravediggers, had to pretend to have dug a hole that just wasn't there. Worse than that, without a grave there could be no skull of Yorick over which Hamlet could mourn.

'And that was when Peter's acting skills really came to the fore,' Finlay told me. 'He stood there, said the lines, and I don't think anyone in the audience could tell that anything had gone wrong.' That indeed was acting. In an attempt to add a sinister touch to his own performance, Frank Finlay took to wearing two contact lenses in one eye, which made him practically blind in it, but caused him to stumble—as he intended—when he moved.

He varied the eye from night to night. O'Toole loved this bit of the business. Every night, he sidled up to the gravedigger and out of the corner of his mouth, sounding for all the world like an Irish Long John Silver, he would ask: 'Which eye is it tonight?'

As always, Peter sought inspiration where he could find it. Thinking about graveyards, he walked around Highgate cemetery. It was one of those occasions of coincidence actors never cease to love talking about. A grave was being dug when he was there. He discovered that it was being readied for the body of an actress whom he knew.

The play was fully booked for three months before opening night, but that didn't impress the men who were supposed to guide public taste. *The Times* described it as a 'routine performance of *Hamlet*' and its anonymous critic wrote: 'Mr O'Toole, like Olivier, is an electrifyingly outgoing actor and it is a surprise to see him make his first appearance from a pit in the forestage with his features twisted into the conventional pattern of introspective melancholy.

'Nothing that follows persuades one that his temperament is in any way engaged in this state of mind. His hollow laughs, lachrymose delivery and dejected stance all seem imposed from without and when he escapes into action, his relief is obvious. But even here his playing is conventional. In the antic scene, he adopts the brittle staccato rasp which is the stock-in-trade of all Hamlets . . .'

In the *Daily Express,* Herbert Kretzmer described O'Toole as looking like a 'blond Beatle' taking the play 'at a pace that borders on the exuberant. The scene in his mother's bedchamber, for example, in which he chastises her iniquitous haste in remarrying so soon after her husband's death is accompanied by such shouting and screaming as to put one in mind of some evangelical rabble-rouser at Speakers' Corner!

'It is Hamlet,' he wrote, 'who disappoints our highest expectations. We observe his anguish but remain obstinately unmoved. We hear his lamentations but our tears remain unshed. It is a performance of great technical skill and authority. But it lacks the final dimension of pity and self disgust that should, but does not, involve our fullest sympathies.'

After some of the things written about his work in recent years that made painful reading indeed.

Milton Shulman said he found Peter's performance 'superb', but his doubts would previously have been enough to get Peter in search of the nearest bottle. Shulman declared: 'Another mistake may have been Peter O'Toole's interpretation of Hamlet as an Elizabethan Jimmy Porter. Although it is possible to find a common denominator between Hamlet's view that his time was out of joint and our own angry young men feeling our own world is all wrong the similarity ends there.

'Hamlet, unlike Jimmy Porter, had a specific concrete direct motivation for his anger, his indecision, his need for action, and he wanted revenge. If his father had been alive and healthy there would have been no play. But O'Toole whose passionate reading of the lines is superb, seems to be making revenge an almost supplementary justification for his deeds . . . And while admiring O'Toole's virile, pulsating performance we are left bewildered about the true purpose of all the sound and fury.'

There were times when Peter might have hoped that the ground would open up to swallow him while on stage in *Hamlet*. As he said afterwards, he had learnt nothing from his performance in the part at Bristol and forgotten everything. What he has never forgotten—or forgiven himself for—is succumbing to the torment that play brought. In his *Playboy* interview the following year, he said: 'I'm hooked on Larry Olivier. I mean he's done it. He's sat on the top of Everest and waved down at the Sherpas. He speaks from Olympian authority and I think he bridles that authority admirably. I know lesser farts in bigger organisations who brandish their puny accomplishments like a club.

'But I'm not sure he ought to be running the National Theatre. Larry's business is acting. He belongs in the stable as head stallion. I don't think he's got a great deal to contribute as a director. In *Hamlet* I wandered amazed among scenic flyovers and trumpets. I didn't know where I was. I only did it because I was flattered out of my trousers.'

It was another example of Peter's unique command of the English language—a gift for conjuring words that flow as easily as if they had been penned for him in a script, mixing poetry with the words of a builder's labourer. Few people can do it either as effectively or unaffectedly.

It was said that his Hamlet had been infinitely more tragic than Shakespeare had intended. That was hardly true. A later experience on the same stage with the same playwright would show just how tragic things could be.

Eight

THERE WERE BRIGHT spots along the way. In June 1963, Peter took a heavily pregnant Sian back to Dublin. Another baby was due and he was determined that this one would arrive well and truly Irish. Their second daughter, a 'real colleen', the Press couldn't help declaring, was named Pat after her grandfather.

It was a happy family, made even more so by the fact that Peter had just received a consolation prize. He may not yet have won the Oscar, but the British Film Academy had named him Best Actor of the Year. The only trouble was that the nomination was for *Lawrence,* the part that was serving to haunt him still. It is interesting to speculate whether he would have felt the same way about *Hamlet* had it worked as well.

Having failed to succeed where he himself wanted to most, he set about consoling himself with another game of checkers. It was time to go travelling, to make more money—and more mistakes. Peter O'Toole, the 'retired Christian' has, to his everlasting credit, never been frightened of admitting those mistakes.

In fact, he does so as if part of a religious exercise; a substitute for confession, a hairshirt to be worn under the green velvet jacket he put on for posh occasions like signing up with producers or giving interviews.

Before very long, he would admit that *Lord Jim* was just one of those mistakes, although it was chosen for the 1964 Royal Film Performance—another great honour—but as experience has shown, no yardstick of artistic superiority in

105

itself. There was a time, however, when the movie first opened in New York and in London, too, when standing-room only signs went up outside the box offices. It didn't last. The film, based on Joseph Conrad's story, was terrible.

It was shot in Cambodia, a place that Peter didn't exactly love. Peter himself complained at one stage during filming that the crew was being exploited by the local politicians. He even accused them of wholesale theft of the crew's equipment and personal belongings. When he reported finding a snake in his soup, the country's leader Prince Sihanouk banned him from ever returning, an eventuality that was exceedingly unlikely. The Prince went on radio to say that he was acting because 'that sort of thing tends to make the tourists nervous'.

He and Sian, who came along for the trip with the children, were themselves fairly nervous much of the time. The war fever which would soon burst out into the horrors of neighbouring Vietnam was already bubbling and embassies were constantly being sacked. The O'Tooles once found themselves in the midst of one such example of revolutionary fervour and found refuge huddling together in a public lavatory. But, he said, it wasn't as stressful as playing at Stratford.

It was not a sentiment necessarily shared by the rest of the crew. When scenes had to be shot on Lord Jim's barge, director Richard Brooks—who wrote the screenplay—and the rest of the crew just had to hope that the river current wouldn't be so strong that it would take them into Red Chinese waters.

Things improved immensely when the crew moved to Hong Kong. But whether Peter felt he had seen too much exploitation of the workers while in Cambodia, or was simply in a mood to be bloody-minded, the old iconoclastic O'Toole of RADA and Bristol was reborn. James Mason told me about one incident which had the *Lord Jim* crowd roaring for days—and had the staff of the plush Peninsula Hotel seething.

The hotel is one of the grandest places in the world. Rolls Royce's sweep up to its doors; flunkeys appear at every corner. It is the lush life for rich people. Peter found something inately offensive in all that. 'So,' Mason told me, remembering the time, 'Peter decided to do something about it. He went downstairs into the street and brought a rickshaw man into the hotel. He then took him into his room and spent the evening talking to him.' No doubt also plying the amazed Oriental with immoderate quantities of booze.

There were delights offered in the hotel that Peter did appreciate. 'He loved the massages that the place specialised in,' James Mason added. 'He persuaded me to have one, too. I think he thought I was a cissy if I didn't go along with the idea. And that's why I had one.' It was not Mr Mason's idea of fun. Nor, alas, was much about the film.

It was a terribly complicated story, about a sailor searching for truth, working with slaves and getting involved in a homosexual rape. Again, the word 'boring' cropped up in reviews. Afterwards, Peter said he would have preferred to have played the subsidiary role that went to Mason. But neither Columbia nor Jules Buck—it was jointly a Keep production—would agree to that. They thought that the simple, sullen, leading character was the only one who merited the investment that Peter O'Toole represented.

The trouble was that Jim was inarticulate—a characteristic that even O'Toole found difficult to master. At the time the film was made, however, he remained loyal to the team. 'I love playing inarticulates,' he said having completed the fifth take of two sentences mumbled across a smoke-filled bar to Akim Tamiroff and Paul Lukas. 'It's a great challenge.' A greater one would have been to face the script and say that Jim wasn't the man for him.

As he explained many years later: 'Lawrence always knew exactly what he was about and could state it precisely. King Henry in *Becket* was bubbling over all the time. But with Jim, talking is like lowering a bucket down a deep well.

It takes a long time to come up. And when it does, you're not sure what's in it.'

He may have been another crazy mixed-up kid—to adopt the vernacular of the time the film was made—but his inability to communicate was just too much. 'When I play reflective types, I tend to reflect myself right off the screen,' he explained at the time. 'It was a mistake, I let everyone down. It would have been better with someone else.'

Now he wanted to do something very different. When further tentative enquiries came from Warner Brothers' Burbank studios asking if he would be available for *My Fair Lady*, he said, 'Certainly. I'd love to play Alfred Doolittle . . . I'm exactly the Professor Higgins type. Very Shavian. A bit violent with blond hair and blue eyes. Basically, Prof. Higgins was a bully.' But that was the last he heard of it.

But it wasn't the end of the *Lord Jim* saga. Yes, he agreed—and consenting to Keep Films suggestions was usually in his own interest—he would do a publicity tour for the film in Japan and then America. It would have been a fairly good idea had he managed his life a bit more sensibly.

He doesn't like flying at the best of times—'I can't believe all that tonnage can float in the air'—and the traumas of the flight from Tokyo, over the North Pole, were greater than he had estimated.

The plane landed en route at Anchorage in Alaska, where he did his digestion no good at all with a dish of chilli. After taking off, Anchorage was hit by a massive earthquake. There would be another in his own life soon afterwards. He arrived in New York to begin a marathon of interviews on radio stations and TV chat shows. He thought he coped pretty well on Channel 13, the public broadcasting service. For an hour, he dealt with an interviewer who knew his job exceedingly well, bringing from Peter both laughter and tears with a lot of other emotions in between.

He certainly thought he had coped well enough not to be frightened of the biggest television programme of them all, Johnny Carson's 'Tonight' show. If he had done nothing else since crossing the Pacific, this was the one that mattered in terms of publicity value and personal prestige.

Frequently a nauseating mixture of back-slapping syrupy singers, coaxing talking dogs and unbelievably bad jokes that bring the house down, Johnny Carson's show, nevertheless, has the biggest ratings in America. O'Toole just had to be good. But he was embarrassingly dreadful.

As Carson greeted the star, it was clear that Peter was under some very heavy weather. His always pasty pallor looked positively death-like on the nation's colour TV screens. His face was lined and, to make things even worse, he wore a pair of very dark glasses. Carson asked him a question and he didn't seem to understand it. A laugh, a cough from the host and another question. Barely two words could be strung together. It was as if the inarticulate Lord Jim had entered the O'Toole bloodstream like Damian in *The Omen*.

And then, Peter put up a finger as though to answer a question—and fell over. His glasses snapped in two; the lenses smashed.

He flew home the next day—'in a box', he said.

The mistakes continued, although Peter worked hard to make sure they had limited effect. The man who had been 'luxuriously broke' was now looking for more ways of lining his nest, and decided that another film was the best way of doing it. The Higgins role in *My Fair Lady* went to Rex Harrison, but O'Toole found his next part in *The Bible*—or rather John Huston's interpretation of the Genesis story. When one tries to understand Huston's casting of O'Toole, it is possible to suspect a somewhat jaundiced view of Holy Writ on the part of the veteran director. Peter played three angels.

The Bible was written—not counting the original author that is—by Christopher Fry, but as a film it was a plodding disaster. It was one of those times when a cinemagoer might have felt tempted to say: 'Saw the picture. Preferred the book.'

Peter was only working on the film for five days, but John Hutson told me that he thought his contribution was the best in the picture. 'It was undoubtedly the best part of the film,' he said. 'I thought he was excellent in his scenes. There is a clarity in his work. Of course, every fine actor is only himself and can't be anyone else. I got him to play the angels because I could think of no reason why they shouldn't all look alike.'

Huston said that he had seen O'Toole many times. They have houses near each other in Ireland and meet when they are there—'but he was perfectly behaved while working on the film. I have never seen any rumbustuousness or anything like that.' But there was some.

The movie was shot in Rome, where Peter displayed his somewhat less than angelic true self by declaring war on a vital section of La Dolce Vita. At three o'clock in the morning, he swiped one of the paparazzi street photographers and ended up in jail.

For that gesture, on behalf of celebrities the world over, he probably earned the undying gratitude of a range of personalities from the then Jackie Kennedy to Elizabeth Taylor. But it was an unpleasant enough experience for him to vow never to work in the Italian capital again.

It happened as Peter's party—it included Albert Finney, actress Barbara Steele and a former champion boxer named Dave Cowley—left the Café de Paris. As they walked to a car, a young photographer named Lino Barillari pushed his way in front of them and started snapping as he reversed two or three paces ahead along the pavement.

That was when the O'Toole ire was raised and he decided he had had enough. He struck out with his right fist into the photographer's face, sending Signor Barillari on to his back. Peter had, in fact, knocked him out.

All the time, words of encouragement were being shouted at the prostrate photographer by the crowds who, despite the time, were still walking the Via Veneto. The paparazzi helped to give the fashionable thoroughfare its image and none of them seemed to want to spoil that view.

Peter and Miss Steele were then taken off to the nearest police station and closely questioned for more than two hours. As it turned out, Lino Barillari was still a minor, so his mother, smelling a fortune in the shape of an international film star, decided to sue and asked for O'Toole's passport to be surrendered. In the end he went on 'trial'—a hearing conducted by the cameramen themselves out in the open on the Via Veneto. Peter went along to the session to see fair play. He was found 'guilty' and sentenced to pay a sum to charity. He wrote a cheque to the Italian anti-polio fund.

On another occasion, the carabiniere tried to impound his luggage, but Peter got to hear about it and smuggled himself down the hotel fire escape. Meanwhile, Peter Perkins, Peter's stuntman and stand-in (as near a look-alike as they come), donned the O'Toole raincoat, cap and dark glasses and went the front way.

The police tapped him on the shoulder—and had to apologise. A Peter O'Toole double looking as though he had plenty to hide turned out to be the perfect decoy. Since Peter was still wearing the angels' beard, no one recognised him.

But the paparazzi kept on trying. Soon afterwards, Peter and Perkins were having a drink in the O'Toole suite when the door burst open, followed by a half-naked blonde who flung herself at Peter's feet. He managed to jump into the next room just before a posse of photographers followed her in.

Some may have said it would have been nothing less than poetic justice if he had been caught. He himself was using his share of paparazzi tactics. Richard Burton was working on an adjoining film set. In one important scene, he was supposed to be set on by a pair of drunks. O'Toole got one of them to let him be a substitute. As Burton wrestled with the men, Peter looked into his eyes and said in perfect Welsh (provided for him by Sian): 'I charge a hundred dollars a day for crowd scenes.'

That trip to Rome was not a totally negative experience. The Italian film industry awarded him a David—the local equivalent of an Oscar—as the best foreign actor of the year—for *Lawrence of Arabia*. More approval, too, came for his action on the Via Veneto. A number of high society figures in Rome decided to lobby Members of Parliament in the hope that they would outlaw the paparazzi. They talked about it—and are still talking. Peter, meanwhile, could not wait to decide what was coming next in his career. He said he fancied playing comedy for the first time.

He made *What's New Pussycat?,* a highly profitable sex comedy written by and co-starring the young and virtually untested Woody Allen. Peter Sellers shared the billing with him and a string of beautiful girls—Ursula Andress, Romy Shneider and Paula Prentiss.

It made money, aided in no small way by a catchy title that for a time entered the public vocabulary on both sides of the Atlantic, and by a theme song by the prolific Burt Bacharach and Hal David.

The film owed more to bedroom farce than comedy. It was an anarchic, Marxist (Groucho Marx, that is) story in which Peter ran from bed to bed, and Sellers was his mad psychoanalyst, in a wig that Olivier might have left behind on the floor of his *Richard III* set. There were rumours that Peter's role was based on the character of Warren Beatty. Not true, he said. It was all himself from beginning to end. And oh those marvellous girls! It made a change, he liked to say, from having to pretend to be in love with either a camel or the Truth.

Critic John Simon wrote: 'Unfortunately for all concerned, to make something enjoyably dirty a lot of taste is required.'

One of the factors that went wrong was that Peter, for all his RADA and Bristol experience, had never done much in the way of improvisation before and that was what Woody Allen now talked him into doing, with Peter Sellers' approval. The idea was that Allen would study the best bits of improvisation and fashion them into the script. It might have been an interesting experience, except that Sellers and Allen disliked each other profoundly.

The three men sat in one room just looking at each other, while in the room next door were the three beautiful women

Before the nose job. The 'magnificent O'Toole hooter' in *Man and Superman* at Bristol, 1958, with Wendy Williams (Bristol Old Vic)

They say that his tramp in *Waiting for Godot* (extreme right) in 1957 was one of the great moments of O'Toole's time at Bristol (Bristol Old Vic)

The General in *Romanoff and Juliet,* Bristol, November 1957, with Barry Wilsher (Bristol Old Vic)

The young Peter O'Toole in his first screen role – *The Savage Innocents*, 1959. Another actor dubbed his voice (National Film Archive)

Above: Filming *Lawrence of Arabia*, Peter shows the camel who's boss (National Film Archive)

Right: The real Lawrence (National Film Archive)

Lawrence, O'Toole style (National Film Archive)

The London critics said it. Peter O'Toole was the Actor of the Year. Here he receives
the Evening Standard Drama Award in 1963 (BBC Hulton Picture Library)

Left: The King in *Becket,* 1964 (National Film Archive)

Below: Becket. Both Peter and Sian would say they hated working together, but when they did they looked superb (National Film Archive)

Welcome home. Sian with baby Kate and Peter arriving at London's Heathrow Airport from New York, March 1964 (BBC Hulton Picture Library)

The house in Heath Street, Hampstead (BBC Hulton Picture Library)

Night of the Generals, 1966 – the haunted look as O'Toole receives the salute of John Gregson (National Film Archive)

Hats off for Mr Chips. Peter and the boys at Sherborne School, 1968, in *Goodbye Mr Chips* (BBC Hulton Picture Library)

Above: With Katharine Hepburn in *The Lion in Winter,* 1968 (National Film Archive)

Right: Playing Napoleon? No, he said, just thinking about 'poor bloody Ireland' – 1971 (BBC Hulton Picture Library)

The mad peer from *The Ruling Class*, 1971 (National Film Archive)

In bed with Elizabeth Taylor – the 'perk' for making *Under Milk Wood* with the Burtons – 1971 (National Film Archive)

Back at the Bristol he loves – in *Uncle Vanya*, 1973 (Bristol Old Vic)

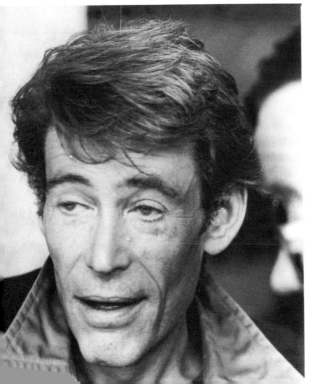

Above: Peter and Sian at Hampstead shortly before he went into the Royal Free Hospital in June 1973. The beard was for the part of Judas – which he would never play. Nobody yet knew that he and Sian were already separate (BBC Hulton Picture Library)

Left: Sickness had plainly taken its toll when this picture was taken in October 1977 (BBC Hulton Picture Library)

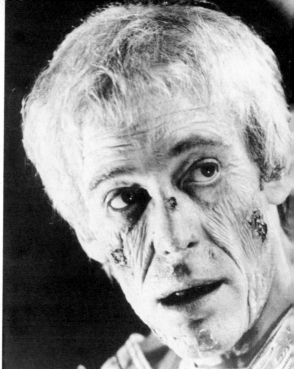

Above: The lean and haggard look in *Caligula* (National Film Archive)

Left: Fluffy slippers and a mug of coffee. All that newspapermen were allowed to see of O'Toole on the morning after the night before – September 198 (BBC Hulton Picture Library)

Right: Is this disaster I see before me? With Frances Tomelty as Lady Macbeth, 1980 (BBC Hulton Picture Library)

Below: Photocall for *Macbeth.* August 1980 – before the Battle of Waterloo Road (BBC Hulton Picture Library)

all nurturing the same hope—to find a way of scratching each others' eyes out.

The film was made in France. Peter turned down the suggestion that it should be worked over in Rome—he wasn't going to do that again—and took every conceivable opportunity to inform the municipality of the Italian capital that he was personally responsible for withdrawing three million dollars' worth of business from their city. He enjoyed making the film—particularly working with Sellers.

It was a time to laugh—and to tease. When he was introduced to a heavily pregnant Britt Ekland, then Sellers's wife, he said to her in a serious, sympathetic voice: 'Isn't it shocking. You've only known him a little while and he's got you into trouble already.'

O'Toole had been wanting to make a comedy for a long time. But he felt inhibited playing farce with 'the funniest man alive', he told Charles Hamblett when it was all over.

The pressures of it all extended beyond the film set. The volatile O'Toole spirit couldn't be contained whenever the occasion arose and trouble seemed to seek him out. A night club he visited had one of the strangest traditions in any country. Every night a policeman visits the club and becomes the principal cabaret attraction. He is plied with as much brandy as he can take and then invited to dance while the customers shout and boo. As the policeman drank, danced and was jeered at, all Peter could think of was a poor hooker he'd seen earlier in the week being beaten up by two gendarmes. Any sense of enjoyment soon turned to anger, and O'Toole joined the fray. He jumped on the gendarme and brought him down on the floor. By the time it was all over, he was satisfied that the man in blue was in no state to use his truncheon on any other woman of the street. 'I hate violence,' he told Hamblett. 'But most of all, I hate juridical violence. It's so cold-blooded.'

Back in England, he was planning his next move. He drove from place to place, now in a Rolls Royce and joked to the hundreds of people who fell in awe on every Peter O'Toole sentence about the way his life had changed—and about Rome, Paris and the thought of Cambodia which still made him shudder every time he thought of the place.

Politics concerned him, too. He gave everyone of voting age in the O'Toole household precise instructions to vote in the 1964 General Election. And, he said, it had to be for Harold Wilson's Labour Party. At that time, he was telling Kenneth Tynan: 'I'm a total, wedded, bedded, bedrock, ocean-going, copper-bottomed triple-distilled Socialist . . . I insisted that everyone . . . vote Labour, even though I knew it would mean I'd be taxed to the bollocks. The only objection came from my driver. "Sack me, if you like," he said, "but I'm Conservative." And he went off in the Rolls and voted Tory.'

Not long afterwards, he was to say that there was nothing like a little wealth to rub off the socialism.

He was also very interested in women. Sian, he told those adoring throngs, was wonderful—'and I mean it, the best actress in Britain'. He loved her greatly, but he could not possibly be faithful to her.

'Marriage is an impossible institution,' he told the *New York Times*. 'I can't be expected to stay in the same room, to remain faithful for ever. This notion of two people being bound to each other can't be legislated. When a marriage works, it's a complete accident, a delightful shock.

'People are not held together by contract, they are held together by mutual esteem. And I'm very fond of Sian.'

There had been talk for a long time about them doing a play together. It was an idea Peter resisted. He didn't think they worked well together—although she had played his wife in *Becket*, simply, she said, because they wanted someone who could read music and speak Welsh.

They were inclined to be hyper-critical of each other's work. But at London's Piccadilly Theatre in June 1965, they took the risk in a play that not only made their relationship appear to be idyllic but seemed to be a return to the Peter O'Toole standards of old.

In *Ride A Cock Horse,* he was brilliant. Sian played his mistress. Barbara Jefford and Wendy Craig were in the play too, helping him go through the fantasies of making love to both his wife and a girlfriend in addition to the mistress.

Peter was not just the star of the play, but so vitally important to its success that he would have in his hands the fate of other actors.

Before the run began he asked for cuts. It was impossibly long, he declared. Cuts were made and approved by him. And then he made a discovery. By losing fifteen minutes at one stage of the story a young actress called Judy Wilson was losing her entire part. 'We can't do that,' he said. 'Put it back.'

'I'll never forget that or stop being grateful to Peter,' Miss Wilson told me.

'I only had four lines, as the au-pair Ingrid, as well as understudying Wendy Craig. His action was such a lovely thing to do. But somehow I was always very shy of Peter.'

He worried a great deal about working with Sian in the play. It was risking divorce every night—like a man teaching his wife to drive. He and Sian certainly had no ambition to be like the Burtons or the Lunts. They both knew that in addition to the hard grind of perfecting a part, there was the worry, perhaps only subconscious, about the effect each was having on the other. And that took much out of both of them.

They would joke about it, but the element of truth could sometimes hurt. As Peter said at the time: 'Before I start work on a film or play, I walk around like a ghost not talking to anyone.'

'Now at home, there are two of us. And one of us is likely to wake up at three in the morning, nudge the other and say: "Now you know when you make that move . . ." '

But there were obvious compensations, such as knowing that Sian would be around to push him out of the house on time. At a time when he was only getting about an hour's sleep a night, helped along by sleeping pills, her encouragement was vital.

115

He never wore a watch, but at 6.30 he knew the time in the same way that a cockerel knew when to crow in the morning. It was an hour from curtain up, and he would never miss an opening curtain in his life, even when in love. When he was far away from a live theatre, at 6.30 some part of his body would twitch, telling him that things were beginning to hum at the back of every stage in the West End and the provinces.

(He didn't carry a key to his front door either; 'I just hope some bastard's going to be in,' he said once.)

Every night, he was on stage at the Piccadilly for two and a half hours, barely leaving the 'boards' throughout the time the curtain was up. It took its toll. After weeks of packing in full houses, he began to feel ill. Abdominal pains were becoming unbearable, undoubtedly the result of living life the way he felt it should be lived, irrespective of the judgment of any doctors.

Peter didn't stay in the play for as long as he expected. Two weeks before it was due to end, he was taken off to hospital with a chest infection. *Ride A Cock Horse* closed at the same time.

All that drink, all that Iron Guts stuff, to say nothing of the sleeping pills, were taking their inevitable toll. He was told to pack it all in or die. So he and Sian went away for a holiday, but the drinking didn't stop. If he couldn't live on his terms, then he wasn't interested.

It was a time in his life when he was having to ask himself where he was going to go next. In fact, it was the question that now seemed to crop up more at interviews than any other. He had numerous ideas, few of which would materialise. First he was going to get his health better. Then he was off to Paris to make two films, one with Audrey Hepburn called *How To Steal A Million,* the other about the Nazis in Warsaw and called *The Night of the Generals.* Both became realities. Other ideas did not. He wanted to play the Duke of Wellington, and he was all but signed for a film to be called *Waterloo,* with Richard Burton playing Napoleon. The film did materialise, but not with them. Christopher Plummer—

once more substituting for Peter—took the Wellington role and Rod Steiger played Napoleon.

He fancied himself playing Sherlock Holmes in a new story being worked on by Billy Wilder—*The Private Life of Sherlock Holmes*. The role would eventually go to Robert Stephens. And then there was the story of Will Adams rolling almost uncontrollably through his mind.

Will who? There weren't many people who did know the name, but Peter had the idea and had begun his customary research project. Adams, history has recorded, was the first Englishman to land in Japan—at the same time as Sir Walter Raleigh and Sir Francis Drake were bringing home the spoils to the first Queen Elizabeth. Adams, on the other hand, landed in Japan after being shipwrecked and was befriended by the Emperor whom he taught to build the first ships his country had ever seen. He was the only Elizabethan, said O'Toole, who didn't go to faraway places in order to plunder, and he liked that.

He also had a perfect script—'the finest that's ever breathed'—written by Dalton Trumbo, John Huston was ready to direct and Japan's leading actor Toshiro Mifune was all geared up ready to play in the film with Peter, who was also going to produce.

It was one of those ideas that seemed so marvellous everyone was going all out to make it. And then they started asking why. Is the idea of a man landing in Japan really that exciting to anyone else? Pearl Harbor seemed just about the only commercial thing with a Japanese connection—apart from Madame Butterfly, that is—and the idea reluctantly had to recede into the O'Toole subconscious. Several years later, when he did think again about making the Will Adams story, *Shogun* had come and gone.

It was a similar story with his next Shakespeare idea. He wanted to play King Lear, although many people said he was still too young. But it would be a chance to earn public approval again, doing just the sort of work for which he felt most fitted. He knew exactly how he wanted to play the King, too. Not like Paul Scofield who had won critical plaudits for an interpretation that Peter considered brilliant but 'not like the way the fellow wrote it'. He admired the Scofield performance—by a 'gent who could show us all the way home'. He went home and found himself that night saying the words as Scofield had said them. 'But in the whole conception, I felt there was too much bending. It bent the text.'

In a marvellously revealing analysis of a Shakespearean character, he told Kenneth Tynan how he saw Lear—'an appalling, dotty old man with two daughters who were the original ugly sisters. That's the simple plot premise and the whole play is about undressing, taking off clothing and crowns and titles. Remove these things and you get the "poor, bare, forked animal". That's the theme and Shakespeare has rivers of irony flowing to express it.

'Of course, Shakespeare makes a comment on our times, but you mustn't forget the people he wrote for who knew all about robes and ceremonies. His theatre wasn't only a temple of the arts, it was a corn exchange.'

To date, Peter O'Toole hasn't had the chance to straighten it out.

But he did his best with *How To Steal A Million,* a comedy about high-class robbers. Peter's performance was more than adequate. 'It's a touch of the Cary Grants,' he said.

Grant was an actor he has always admired—perhaps subconsciously it stems from the day he sold him that ice cream at Bristol—and his name tends to crop up in conversation. The ease of a Grant comedy is not to be dismissed—but in that consummate performance is a warning, too. Grant was forever typecast, rarely managing to escape the light, if suave, image. Peter has always considered that as dangerous as never escaping from Lawrence. It is for that precise reason that he has tried to vary his output, even though the lure of riches sometimes distorted the aim.

Despite its title, *How To Steal A Million* did not fit into the work-for-money's sake mould. It could just have been a big success, with a great deal working for the movie. In names alone, it should have stolen more than a million at the box office.

Audrey Hepburn looked beautiful—it was a toss up as to who was the thinner—and there were entertaining performances from Charles Boyer and Hugh Griffith. William Wyler directed, but the critics didn't think he did it terribly well. 'Wyler hasn't got the touch any more,' said the informed *Sight and Sound* magazine. The film, they decided was, 'terribly wordy and slow'.

The Night of the Generals was a different bowl of sauerkraut altogether. It paired Peter with Omar Sharif again, and audiences once more were entitled to feel a need to grip the sides of their seats. Peter himself greeted the role as a total change. No more the romantic twits. No longer the search for understanding. Into the past the white robes of Lawrence. All that was true, except that if you were looking for resemblances the Nazi General Wilhelm Tanx—mad, psychopathic and in charge of the German war machine in Warsaw—did seem to enjoy the blood and carnage in a way that Lawrence would have understood.

William Wyler was wrapping up *How To Steal A Million* while work on *The Night of the Generals* was at full steam. He needed O'Toole to dub a line of dialogue and since both projects were being made in Paris, it was easy for Peter to take an hour or so from one of those interminably boring waiting periods to go to a sound studio in the city and recite the words: 'Ring out wild bells' (the original recording had been submerged under the sound of those wild bells). It was a strange, revealing experience.

There was Peter, dressed as though he were about to welcome Hitler to Nuremberg, supposed to be joyously in love with Audrey Hepburn. There were jackboots in the audience and romance on the screen and it was all but impossible to put the two together. He couldn't even remember the right voice to use.

119

Nigel Stock who worked on *The Night of the Generals* told me it was impossible not to be affected by a Peter O'Toole so obviously at the peak of his form. Another O'Toole characteristic in very strong evidence at the time was the respect for his fellow actors which had shown itself so many times before.

It was while the film was in production that the Bristol Old Vic celebrated its bicentenary. All its 'old boys' and 'old girls' were invited back to drink a toast and reminisce about old times. Val May, the new director of the theatre, had devised a revue telling the story of the Old Vic in the city, which he called 'Sixty Thousand Nights'—for the mathematically-inclined, the number of evenings at which the company had performed. To Peter, for whom Bristol was always an *alma mater* even more significant in his training than RADA, it was like a summons to court. More important, he really wanted to go.

The film's director, Anatole Litvak, agreed that the schedule could be switched around to grant him the chance of going to Bristol. To make things easier for everyone, Peter decided to charter a plane, and took Peter Perkins along for the ride.

Halfway across the Channel, O'Toole thought it would be rather nice to wash the feel of France from his liver. The yearning for a good English pub suddenly became irresistible. The pilot was told to go to London. From Elstree aerodrome, he hired a car to drive the two Peters to his favourite hostelry, the Salisbury, in St Martin's Lane.

Satisfied to the point of extreme happiness, he then asked the landlord to provide him with a couple of crates of champagne, which went with them on the run back to Elstree and then on to Bristol.

Unfortunately for all concerned, the Bristol experience was not totally satisfactory. Peter arrived late; after Princess Marina, Duchess of Kent, had been welcomed and just as the 'old boys' were taking a bow on the stage. Modestly, he found his way to the wings and stood at the back of the 150 or so people on stage.

'He then decided he was going to take us all out for a dinner,' Val May told me. The cellars of Harveys of Bristol sherry emporium were commandeered and 150 people were invited. But it was as though the jackbooted centre of attraction in *The Night of the Generals* had taken charge.

'He refused to allow anyone to leave the table. And when someone did, the man with Peter made very sure he sat down again. "If anyone goes," said O'Toole, "he's a pouff". It all turned rather nasty.'

Nat Brenner said he thought Peter's behaviour was caused simply by his not being very happy with the film he was making. And yet, he left for Paris seemingly in a good mood and more ready than usual to rest on the return journey. Sleep, he decided, was not going to be a problem, even with the prospect of a Channel crossing and the journey to the Paris studios in the offing. Nobody in a French film studio— quite different from the situation in Hollywood or in British pictures, for that matter—is expected to be able to recite lines and make love at six o'clock in the morning. Nothing ever begins before noon. ('And then,' Donald Pleasence, who played another Nazi in the movie, told me, 'Litvak would usually check the lighting and everything else, turn to us and say, "Time for lunch, my children" '.)

The O'Toole optimism in this case, however, had reached the point of carelessness. The two Peters got back to the studio very late. No work could begin, because O'Toole was in all the scenes being shot that day. His lateness was not only costing Sam Spiegel and Columbia a great deal of money, the price of frayed nerves among the cast was a heavy one, too—a fact of which Peter was painfully aware.

As soon as he arrived, he asked for the entire cast, the other stars like Omar Sharif, Tom Courtenay, Donald Pleasence and Nigel Stock, bit players and extras, too, to be assembled. To them all, he said he was extremely sorry.

'I thought that was pretty big,' said Stock.

It was, nevertheless, part of Peter's own individual look at life.

Other stars enjoyed the tycoon life to which they were exposed, the business meetings, the dinners, the breakfasts.

Someone asked Peter for breakfast when he finished making *The Night of the Generals* and he politely refused. 'All I have for breakfast,' he said, 'is a fingernail and a Gauloise.'

The trouble with Peter's reputation as a hellraiser was that people sometimes thought he would make a pretty good breakfast out of them, too. But in 1968 he met his match in the formidable form of Katharine Hepburn.

Nine

SHE BULLIED AND she nagged at him; told him that he drank too much, that he was shortening his life. In return, he filled her car with empty beer and spirit bottles, making her look like a raving alcoholic. But it was a splendid idea, in 1968, to put them together in *The Lion in Winter*. Katharine Hepburn was a wonderful co-star.

If the lion in the form of a Henry II—who had already rid himself of the problems of Thomas à Becket—raised its voice, then Queen Eleanor of Aquitaine roared, too.

It wasn't a story that owed everything to the written history of the Plantagenets. James Goldman, in writing the story, had allowed his imagination to run revolutions around the notion of the bearded King and the older Queen spending Christmas together, and ending up rowing marvellously. Nobody, it was thought, could row better than Peter Seamus O'Toole. Miss Hepburn, drawing on the experience of all those years playing emancipated females on the screen, gave him a good run for his money.

For Peter, playing Henry again was like stepping into a comfortable pair of old slippers. It was a maturer, less confused King now, but he saw the role as a continuation of the one before and it benefited enormously. He was the first to recognise that he also benefited from the company of the woman whom he now christened Old Nags.

She, in turn, called him Pig—and bashed him not a few times when he thought twice about her instructions to put down a bottle. 'I just adore her, even when she does hit me,' he told writer Roderick Mann in the *Sunday Express*.

Their relationship off camera was just right for the roles they played on the screen. The story focused around royal marriage problems. He woos and beds the busty Princess Alais of France (Jane Merrow), while she is banished so that the affair can progress to his satisfaction.

A meeting has been called to discuss the King's plans for his two sons. He thinks it will help relations with France if his beautiful mistress is married to one of his boys—although he can't be certain which. One of them has already cemented relations of a kind with the country over the sea by having an affair with the King. A second has established he'd like nothing better than to murder his old man and the third, to quote the Princess, 'has pimples and smells of compost'.

The Queen arrives in state from her dungeon. 'How dear of you to let me out of jail,' she says as the King bows to kiss her hand.

'It's only for the holidays,' he replies.

The Lion in Winter made a holiday for audiences all over the world, earned Miss Hepburn an Oscar for the second successive year—it followed *Guess Who's Coming To Dinner*, the last movie she made with Spencer Tracy—and got Peter nominated yet again for an Award he didn't win.

In the London *Daily Mirror,* Donald Zec described it as 'an altogether triumphant achievement in picture making'. If it was, it owed a great deal to being one of those occasions when teamwork was seen to count. At Peter's suggestion, most of the supporting cast were unknown young actors he himself had discovered and then passed on for the approval of Miss Hepburn and the director Anthony Harvey—who had himself been recommended by O'Toole.

Harvey had made a film called *Dutchman* which Peter greatly admired, and he had told Katharine so when he went to America to discuss the film with her. He suggested that Miss Hepburn go to see it with him. They found it being shown in a sleazy neighbourhood cinema in New York.

There, among tramps sheltering from the cold and drinking metholated spirits, and couples making love, they picked their director.

They found their other actors in the provincial repertory theatres of England, young men and women who said they were determined to go back to the stage when filming was over.

If Peter felt a slight yearning for kindred spirits, he didn't say so. But he did think the film was essentially a theatrical experience for the cast, as much as he hoped it would be for an audience who may have expected a great deal of medieval colour and grandeur but had to make do, instead, with the smoke-filled, grimy quarters of a King whose bed looked as though it had been part of the furniture of a very run-down brothel.

Because of this theatricality, the first two weeks of rehearsals were spent on the stage of London's Haymarket Theatre. Filming was in France and Ireland. In both places, Peter decided it was necessary to work—both at making a movie and having a good time.

Katharine Hepburn was worried about both these aspects of his life. She liked the way they patently made a good team for the cameras and were obviously respected by the rest of the cast. Thirty-six-year-old O'Toole was thrust deep into middle age by the attitude of some of the young players—'They are treating us like the mother and father of the outfit,' he said at one stage. He only realised how old he felt when one of the cast asked him for some advice on sex.

But the woman who had had some knowledge of what actors can do to themselves when they hit the top, was more concerned with Peter's seemingly less mature attributes. She didn't think he chose the right parts most of the time, she told him. 'You're a bad picker, Pig,' she said. To which he replied, 'Only one flop since I started.' 'Don't argue,' she came back. He then called her 'an old female impersonator', and hoped she would change the subject. When she did and the subject became his drinking, he wasn't any more happy.

But she was a marvellous sparring partner. Once, during the early days of filming, there had been a dispute between the two stars over who had prior claim on a make-up artist. Katharine burst into Peter's dressing room and levelled two sharp punches on his jaw.

The next day Peter turned up for work with his left arm bandaged and in a sling. Both laughed, showing they were still friends. 'She's like a bloody poultice,' he said in the Roderick Mann interview. 'She pulls a performance out of you.'

Once, she almost pulled a finger out of his hand, too—the right one, inevitably. One scene called for Henry to meet his Queen on a barge. As the two boats pulled alongside each other, Peter's little finger was wedged between the two.

That was far from the only mishap while on location. He awoke one night to find his bed on fire—doubtless the result of enjoying one of those Gauloises while thinking about the next day's lines. There was a fire extinguisher in his room, but the sleeping pills and other tablets he had been taking made his eyes foggy and he couldn't read the instructions—or even really make up his mind whether he was actually experiencing the fire or just dreaming. He realised it was for real when a gang of firemen burst into the room. When he saw them, he ran towards the one nearest to him and kissed him wildly on the cheek.

There were other happenings which he very carefully organised—usually for the benefit of other people who, as always, were his bosom buddies for the length of the filming operation.

Filming took place in France in January—so that the winter settings would be totally accurate. Most of the cast were based in the town of Arles, in a luxury hotel convenient for getting to work easily. Peter himself was based nearby at Les Beaux in a hotel that was normally shut for the winter, but which opened specially for him because he knew that it served the best Marseilles-type food and drink in the world. After a few days there, he decided that the time had come to share these delights with the rest of the company at his own expense. They came by the car-load. The stars like Miss Hepburn, the unknowns, the established actors like Nigel Stock, the extras, camera crew and the director.

It was quite an intimidating place at the best of times, that hotel. Situated high on the cliff, it had once been a popular place both for suicides and murders, not a few of which had been unofficial political executions.

The blows this time came in a somewhat different form. Peter had arranged for the maitre d' to serve what was generally regarded as the best bouillabaisse in France, together with a bottle or two of the local white wine. The more astute among his guests may have noted that Peter, who never ate much anyway, was eating even less than usual. More significantly, he was keeping away from the booze. They may have thought that he was at last preparing himself for a jump on to the wagon. His scheme was much more devious, however.

The wine tasted marvellous, except that it didn't seem to have much effect. You just wanted to pour another one. It was much stronger than anyone imagined and Peter knew it. He sat by, thoroughly enjoying the spectacle. Nigel Stock recalled for me: 'After just three glasses his business manager, wearing a black jacket and striped trousers, was doing a Cossack dance on his haunches in the middle of the floor.

'None of us had more than he did but we were all positively paralytic. Peter just sat there looking on and enjoying it. It was a night to remember, I can assure you. It was that Peter O'Toole mischievousness which you just had to know how to take.'

Not everyone took him quite so kindly.

One of the reasons why he wasn't staying at the same hotel as everyone else was because he had been invited to leave by the management—after a series of what producer Joseph E. Levine of AVCO Embassy Productions called 'drunken orgies', in which he used obscene language.

It was all too much for the producers who complained that O'Toole was adding to these difficulties by coming late to the set in the morning. When it was all over, Mr Levine and executive vice president, Leonard Lightstone, decided to with-hold some of Peter's money—a fee of $750,000 plus ten percent of the profits. The firm withheld $200,000 of this because, they said, his antics reflected adversely on the film. His behaviour, they pointed out, amounted to a breach of contract. He had failed 'to conduct himself in accordance with commonly-accepted public conventions and morals'—a catch-all phrase that had worried the Hollywood acting community for generations.

Peter and Jules Buck—once more the deal had been with Keep Films—took the matter to court in New York, where Supreme Court Justice Gerald Culkin ruled that Peter's behaviour was no excuse for penalising him financially. The money, he said, had to be paid. Jules Buck, who had spent quite a time himself trying to tame Peter's excesses, was relieved. 'He's not really that much of a hellraiser,' he said with a face that had 'you could have fooled me' written all over it. 'He is very highly-charged emotionally and he occasionally goes on a bender. But don't we all?' It was a question that begged for reassurance.

Clearly, Sian had faced similar difficulties. She did agree that it was part of him. Peter was a man of many moods. One of their joint decisions was still to try not to work together. 'We loathe working with each other. It's a quick way to the divorce court. I'm always afraid he's going to dry and he's always waiting for me to do something wrong. We're both so nervy of each other, we can't possibly act.'

But of all his problems, that was rarely one of them. He even made brave efforts at acting as a nobody. He would go to smart West End restaurants for lunch or even tea wearing a battered green hat, and no one would do more than give him a quizzical glance—more because of the hat than because he had been recognised.

He didn't really want too much recognition in Hampstead either. It was impossible to enter the house without coming up against a considerable security barrier, including having to announce your name and business into a microphone—quite a rarity at the time.

Burglars did once manage to get in, however. They got away with the two paintings by Jack Yeats that Hal Wallis had given him. They were worth a total of about £1,500, but they brought back memories of *Becket,* were Irish, and held more sentimental value in a house that was gradually taking on the quality of a Dublin in exile—with a generous injection of theatre, too.

His inner sanctum-den he called the Marcus Luccicos Room, an 'in joke', for Luccicos is a character in *Othello* who never appears. The Senate calls for him urgently but after he fails to answer, the character disappears from the action altogether. It was as though the room was given the name as a kind of warning to himself. How easy, indeed, it is for the mighty to fall.

If *The Lion in Winter* had made him feel middle aged, the question of advancing years now bothered him more and more. Once, he asked Sian how old he was, and when she told him he was close to forty, he looked at her in mock disgust and shouted, 'Lying whore!' It was a good enough reason to pour another drink.

Not that he needed reasons, much to the anguish of his doctors who were now suggesting that he try to find other ways to expend his energies. Why was work not enough? One reason could be that he was doing more and more work on the floor of a film studio—and telling people he was only doing it for the money. 'I'm trying to coin it in before all the teeth fall out.' What bothered his friends was that the teeth looked like falling out much sooner than they should. His morning cough was so impressive that he took to recording it for posterity on the tape machine he kept in his den for performances of a different kind. He wouldn't be swayed from having a good time any more than he could have been talked out of going to the Bristol celebrations.

If there was a laugh in it as well as the tip of a bottle he wanted to be along for the ride. One example was when Peter Sellers did his James Bond spoof, *Casino Royale*. O'Toole decided he didn't want to be left out. Like many other performers, he thought the nice thing to do would be to visit the set. In one scene, there were a hundred pipers adding a Gaelic touch to the enterprise. Peter, still something of an expert on the bagpipes, decided to make it one hundred and one. It is one Peter O'Toole film not among those listed in catalogues of his work, but in that scene he can plainly be seen blowing his brains out. He said he just did it for a St Patrick's Day joke and only wishes it had been cut out of the final print.

They were still saying that about the more official O'Toole films, wondering why he didn't follow Katharine Hepburn's advice and be a better 'picker', doing work that matched his brilliant talent.

In 1969, he decided on an even more disastrous course of action than usual. He chose to become a producer—and act in a film at the same time. It is a role other stars have chosen and usually lived to regret. There is a huge conflict of interests involved. Every actor likes his best work to be evident, whether it is an important speech or just a chance of showing the more flattering profile. There is always a risk of a producer-actor either putting too much emphasis on his own work, or sacrificing his performance for the sake of the whole. *Great Catherine,* based on George Bernard Shaw's story of Catherine the Great, was a failure from beginning to end.

I remember talking to Peter about it on the set at Shepperton Studios. He was darting in full costume—like a greyhound smelling an electric hare—from the set to a business meeting and back to the set again. He was sure it was going to be one of the best things he had ever done. But he probably knew then that it wouldn't be. He is a good enough businessman to understand that when you are selling a product you only talk about the good things. He has always been honest enough to admit afterwards when things have gone wrong. And *Great Catherine* was one of those things.

He certainly endeavoured to pull out all the stops. With Jeanne Moreau as the empress, it seemed as though he had a great deal going for the enterprise. 'What do you think of Moreau?' he asked a friend. 'Marvellous,' the friend replied. 'No, I mean what do you think of that jewellery she's wearing?' 'Great,' he said, praising the work of the paste-gem makers. 'It's real, you know,' he said. And it was.

Peter had discovered where some of the Romanoff crown jewels were kept in England and arranged to borrow them. They were so valuable that no publicity could possibly be allowed. Which was a pity. The film could have done with it.

While working on the film, he told journalists: 'I have great hopes for *Great Catherine*. I think it's good.' But his director, Elliot Silverstein, wasn't so sure. He pointed to Peter's additional role in the movie and said: 'I can never be a star's lackey,' and quit. He was replaced by Gordon Flemyng in an atmosphere of total chaos.

Peter was convinced that he would never try to produce another movie himself—and it made him reflect on the industry as it stood at the end of the decade. 'My heart just dribbles out of the bottom of my toes when I think how this film industry works. Get me the director of *Divorce Italian Style* and we'll make a story proving that Rommel was a woman and is now living in South America. That's how it starts. But I'm not going to have anyone messing with our film. No one's going to get work on it with a knife and fork. If it's going to be wrong, I want it to be wrong my way.'

It was, and hardly worked at all—even though Peter's own performance as a British sea captain at the Imperial Court had an anarchic brilliance about it, fed probably by the lingering memories of his own experience in the Royal Navy. There were also charming performances by Jeanne Moreau and Akim Tamiroff and the first appearance by Jack Hawkins since the operation to remove his larynx as a result of cancer.

The trouble was that the film just didn't hang together.

What Peter needed was more exposure to the atmosphere of Ireland. And he was going to get it the way he wanted most—back on the stage.

131

Ten

PETER ONCE SAID that he fancied himself as a latter-day
Errol Flynn. It was a fair comparison, although O'Toole had
more talent in his eyes alone than Flynn had in his whole
body. But there was the same kind of charisma. The same
charm, which one could, if searching for psychological roots,
put down in each case to an Irish background—Flynn was
born in Tasmania but his father was Irish and Warner Brothers would always say Errol was, too; it sounded romantic.
There was also the same tendency to live dangerously.

The difference was that as he entered his forties Flynn
would say that it didn't matter if he died tomorrow. He had
lived at least twice. Like Flynn, O'Toole has grabbed everything available to him and sampled the fun while earning a
fortune. But unlike Errol at the same age, he would not have
been content if it all ended the next day. There was still a
great deal more to do, and at the risk of contradicting himself
along the way, he didn't mind who knew it.

The actor who had said that it was unnatural for man to
remain monogamous was now declaring that he valued his
marriage above all else—and if you did that, you didn't play
around. Sian, too, valued what they had. Their success came
from appreciating their own individual qualities, which was
another reason why it wasn't good for them to work together.
More than that, she said, they allowed each other a degree of
privacy which was important in marriage. She had never seen
Peter shave, she said. He had never seen her put on her
make-up.

If they didn't like working together, unless pressed, they followed each other's careers avidly. Sian would watch her 'Pete' filming, Peter wouldn't miss any of her plays. It was a fact that everyone in the business got to know about them; an easy reason for teasing.

When Sian was in the play *Gentle Jack,* Peter was there to cheer her on at the West End first night. He met another member of the cast on the staircase as, striding three steps at a time, he moved towards her dressing room. Michael Bryant, who was later to play with O'Toole in *Goodbye Mr Chips,* thought it was a moment for compliments. 'Sian acts better than you ever could,' said Bryant basking in the glory of a cheering first night audience. It was a joke and Peter took it as one—which meant that he had to reply in kind. It was an answer that would have made him an instant member of the Errol Flynn roustabouts.

'You cunt,' said Peter, without making any obvious move to search for words—for the less obvious ones were coming very rapidly—'I've got more hairs on my cock than you've got on your head.'

Bryant laughed—as he was supposed to do. And never forgot it. For Peter, it was simply his way of showing he was still one of the boys. But that didn't mean he was any less the devoted head of what people thought was a very nice family.

In 1969, he thought it would be a good idea to ignore Noël Coward's advice to Mrs Worthington and put his daughter on stage, or at least in films. Kate had a small part, with Sian, in the film *Laughter In The Dark.* 'I need the money,' said Peter afterwards. 'I don't intend to make an actress of her necessarily.'

Her previous theatrical experience had been limited to a school nativity play when, as he said, she 'got religious', which probably resulted from going to a Catholic school. She came home and told her parents she had been in an 'activity play in which Jesus Kite was killed at the crossings'. But, he said, she was a very serious and introspective young lady. At ten years old, she was already middle-aged. Pat, on the other hand, was 'very Irish and extrovert'. In fact, Peter would say that it was Pat who took after him.

Peter's love for his children is plain. It comes through whenever he speaks about them and he does that often enough. It is an inbred condition, almost a sub-conscious attempt to promote the kind of relationship that he had with his own parents—if without the tensions that come from running the gauntlet of the racetracks.

Every now and again, Peter would think about politics. As a child, on holiday in Ireland, he had run from one town to the next thrilled at the effects of the dropping of the first atomic bomb at Hiroshima. He has neither forgotten that joy nor forgiven it. He marched in the 'ban-the-bomb' demonstrations from London to the British atomic research centre at Aldermaston, and continued to support the Campaign for Nuclear Disarmament.

Meanwhile, Peter's drinking habits weren't improving. Doctors told him to lay off drink and he told them he had no intention of doing so—yet. There were stomach pains and still more operations on his eyes. But he wasn't going to let any of that curtail what he had in mind for himself. He said that he had known since he was twenty that he would one day be seriously ill, so there was no point in failing to enjoy himself while he could.

In 1969, he decided that that enjoyment was going to come principally from going back on stage. The man who did his work on the screen because of the money was proving that there were other things in life, too. And many of these seemed to depend on being in Ireland. He may have spent those formative years of his life in Leeds and his natural voice—as distinct from most of the ones he used on the screen or on stage—still had those very distinct Yorkshire nuances to it, but it was Irish he felt. Now he had a yearning to combine his work with his heritage.

He had plans to repeat his considerable success at Dublin's Gaiety Theatre three years earlier, when he played Jack Boyle in *Juno and the Paycock*. He wouldn't do the same play

134

again, but it would be a gesture to Ireland. And there was a film to do in the country, too.

Country Dance, based on a short story by James Kennaway, was set in Scotland. But since the Wicklow Mountains bore an uncanny resemblance to the heights of Perthshire and there were studios readily available in Dublin and none at all in Scotland, it met Peter's idea of perfection precisely.

It was a story that plainly tickled his fancy. The character he played was a crazy alcoholic, who had an incestuous relationship with his sister—played by Susannah York, who was capable of being fairly spirited herself.

The film's director was J. Lee Thompson, who had made *The Guns of Navarone* and *MacKenna's Gold* among numerous other movies. He was a friend of James Kennaway, and with him and the producer Robert Ginna, had sold the idea to MGM. Now all they had to do was sell it to Peter. The play was based on a series of short stories called *Household Ghosts,* which had been put together under the title *Country Dance,* and was featured at the Edinburgh Festival. The idea for the project appealed to Peter immediately.

That same day, Kennaway had a heart attack while driving his car and was killed.

No one doubted that the project should go ahead, but Peter was determined that it should proceed on his terms. He wanted certain changes and if they were not made, he wasn't interested. A meeting was held at the Dorchester Hotel in Park Lane. Peter surveyed the people present, the director, technical people, writers, Jules Buck. His eye landed on Robert Ginna. 'Out!' he said. 'We don't want any goddam producers here.'

It was not a move calculated to win friends and influence people, least of all his producer. Nevertheless, it turned out to be a happy relationship and all in all a happy movie, with Susannah York and Peter getting on very well with each other and both of them liking their co-star, Michael Craig.

The rural Irish atmosphere had a lot to do with it, too. During his time working there, he met his old friend Joe

O'Connor again. 'It was as though we were at Bristol again. We had three or four wonderful days together,' O'Connor said.

The director and producer told me they only have happy memories of it as well. But they had to know how to treat Peter with what he regarded as the right amount of respect. Peter, on the other hand, had to learn that the director was there with a precise function to fulfil, and it was up to him to smooth his task.

But he showed an active interest in everything. Peter, never renowned for his wardrobe taste—although he will admit to having 'forgotten' to give back a jacket or two he may have borrowed while filming—took the choosing of the clothes for *Country Dance* as his own prerogative. He considered the way the man was dressed to be an intrinsic part of his character.

The movie had a budget of about three million dollars. In 1969, that was fairly minimal. He himself took what was regarded as only a 'token' salary, but after the first production meeting the tokens started multiplying. Like all stars, he insisted on first-class travel. That would have been expected. He also wanted a comfortable car to drive him to and from the various locations. That, too, was anticipated—except that O'Toole had a particular car in mind. He required on his own white Mercedes being flown over to Ireland at the company's expense. More than that, he insisted that Peter Perkins be added to the payroll—another example of his intense loyalty.

With these matters settled, he set about making sure that he was going to do this particular *Country Dance* with all the exuberance of a jig to the accompaniment of a Connemara fiddler.

He told Robert Ginna: 'You know, we're not going to make a buck on this, don't you? But let's have a bloody good time.' And it was a good time very much on Peter's terms. As Ginna told me: 'Peter is rather like a racehorse. If you want a light canter around the park, you don't pick a thoroughbred.

In Peter we had a thoroughbred so we prepared ourselves. Certainly, he could be meddlesome. But he could also be wonderful.'

It was his 'wonderful' idea to use the Harbour Bar on the Bray seashore for a scene. He lived the part the same way he lived all his roles, and because he played an alcoholic in the film, he drank—much, much more than even he usually consumed, although J. Lee Thompson assured me, that he never allowed it to affect his work other than in the way he planned. 'He never held up shooting once.' But for the most part, he enjoyed his research.

He had discovered the Harbour Bar when making *The Lion in Winter* at the same Ardmore studios they were using now. Half the place was occupied by the cameras and lighting and other equipment. In the other half it was business as usual, but with all the Irish beer and liquor signs taken down and Scottish advertisements installed in their place. Actually, there was a reason for using the pub that went beyond simple taste. It was owned by a couple of men named O'Toole—no known relation to Peter, but he had convinced them and himself that they were all of the same Irish blood royal.

'This is where I find my own people, the little people, the real people of Ireland,' he declared proudly. He also found them at the racetrack—where he constantly took members of the crew. When a horse called Country Dance was running, he made sure they all put a bob or two on it. They won enough to keep them happy.

There was another time, in another pub, when the people of Ireland with whom he came into contact were neither little, nor quite so charming. It happened after a poker game at the Shelbourne Hotel in Dublin, where Peter and the other actors were staying. All through the game, he had been consuming a considerable amount of champagne. He was plainly enjoying every second. Among those playing were filmmakers, Peter and John Alonso, who were making a documentary about the making of *Country Dance*. They wanted a scene showing Peter, the consummate insomniac,

137

spending his nights at a pub. Naturally, that wasn't the easiest thing to do at three o'clock in the morning when the decision to look for an all-night establishment was made.

They finally found one in the less salubrious region of Dublin's docks. Even there the landlord, Bernard Markowski, said it was too late. He would not serve the party. Such a statement to Peter was roughly the same as the sound of boos from a theatre audience or a firm refusal by a director to go along with one of his ideas.

Peter reacted with some fairly choice language of his own. At which point, the landlord set his Alsatian dog on his would-be customer. The combined efforts of Ginna and the other members of the party managed to pull Peter away. But he didn't want to be pulled. He was determined to go back, this time to tell the landlord precisely what he thought of him.

The gardai were called—in time to watch Peter administer a superbly executed upper cut to Mr Markowski's jaw, knocking him to the ground and sending the Alsatian fleeing in terror. Peter, Ginna and the filmmakers were carted off to the police station.

After an hour or so, the other members of the crew were released. Peter was incarcerated in the high-security Bridewell Jail, and only released several hours later. 'He had been severely beaten up by the police,' Ginna told me. 'His face was bruised and cut. He had also been bitten by the dog. We had to find a doctor for him in the middle of the night.'

But a couple of hours later he was back on the set—thanks to the ministrations of the make-up department. The next day an excuse was found to film him in dark glasses.

He was later fined thirty pounds for assault. Another charge of using offensive language was dropped. District Judge John Farrel told him: 'Your previous good character has saved you from prison.' Peter, wearing a check suit and horn-rimmed glasses, left court without having given evidence—and doubtless glad that some of his happenings on the other side of the Irish sea had not reached the attention of the judge.

Some of his language on the set was none too choice either. J. Lee Thompson told me that the great thing about Peter's acting before a film camera is the contribution he makes towards the whole filming operation. 'The main function of a director working with Peter O'Toole is to treat his talents as a bargain basement. He will give you all the goods, but you have to select the ones you need. That means you have to be very careful that you choose correctly.'

Of course, O'Toole didn't think much of directors at any time. Even in the theatre, they were a new invention—to protect authors from the whims of the actors. 'Given a good play and a decent set,' he said in a *Playboy* interview, 'you could chain a blue-arsed baboon in the stalls and get what is known as a production.'

Peter thought he knew the man he was playing. A crazy man had to behave crazily. He suggested dialogue that showed his usual intuitive insight into a role. 'But,' said Lee Thompson, 'if I wasn't careful he would go over the top.'

He would jump on tables, prance in a frenzy around the set, wear his trousers back to front. 'The trouble is you are apt to fall in love with some of those crazy things and have to be very careful not to be seduced by the marvellous invent-iveness of his genius—a word I use sparingly, but which in this case is absolutely right. He has a uniqueness.'

But, he said, he understands why other directors have considered him difficult. He didn't like the idea of having some of his most inventive ideas rejected. O'Toole's top would be blown in glorious Technicolor. 'You're a fucking madman,' he called to Lee Thompson after one such rejec-tion. You don't know what you're doing.'

That called for a certain strategy on the director's part. 'If you know he's not going to take things lightly and that nothing comes easily, you have to be very sparing in your rejections.'

But the suggestions were mostly constructive and were received as such. One scene, he suggested, would work bet-ter if he climbed over all the furniture in the kitchen and jumped through the window. He was talked out of that one. 'He hated me,' Lee Thompson said. 'But it was all over the next day. However, he was never the kind of actor who will go through his part intensely and then at the end of it ask you what won the three-thirty. He was much too involved for that.'

And yet, all the time, the parties went on. One of them was organised by Robert Ginna. For this, Peter set up an Irish group, the Chieftians, to play for the evening. In the course of the proceedings, he and Susannah York got into a friendly but heated discussion. To stress his point, Peter took off a boot and threw it in the actress's direction, knowing, of course, that it would miss her. She ducked and the boot sailed past, demolishing the glass-covered bookshelves behind. The argument continued, neither Peter nor the feisty Susannah wanting to let go.

He didn't want to let go of *Country Dance* either. 'I want it to be a tribute to Kennaway,' he said. But as predicted, it didn't make a buck either. In America, the film was restricted to art houses under the title *Brotherly Love*. Its incestuous theme meant it was denied mass television exposure there.

In England, the film came and went, although the critical response was not at all bad. 'Peter O'Toole has a whale of a time,' said *The Times,* 'with a very showy performance, and is just allowed to take over the film by the director, J. Lee Thompson. It is perhaps not badly done, but the problem posed is so special and the people are so tiresome to be with, even for two hours, that it is hard to find much to say in the film's favour.'

But its Irish connection was perhaps enough for its star. And that was why he relished the opportunity, almost immediately afterwards, to be back on stage. By playing at the Gaiety, he was realising both his love for the live theatre, and helping to consummate his love affair with Ireland. Those who went to see *Man and Superman* by perhaps the greatest of all modern Irish dramatists, George Bernard Shaw, were not disappointed. There are some who saw him in that play who think that it was one of his finest productions. For them, he not only sounded as though he were reciting Shaw, he *was* Shaw. His beard and his hair were dyed as red as for the part of John Tanner, the role he had played in Bristol eleven years earlier.

There are some actors who can make their private conversations sound as though they form part of a book or script. Peter, on the other hand, has the gift of making the experience of listening to him on stage feel like the act of eavesdropping on a private chat.

Nigel Stock worked with him again in *Man and Superman*. He played the lawyer Robuck Ramsden and, by all accounts, did it brilliantly. That was precisely the way he described the performance by O'Toole, too.

'Peter has always been an actor of surprise. When he played Tanner in Dublin, it was the finest thing I've ever seen.

'His words just tripped off his tongue. There has never been a Shavian experience like it.'

There had been few theatrical experiences like it, either. Peter wanted his return to Dublin to be perfect and so hedged no bets. He chose his own company. John Hurt played Octavius.

He chose his own director—the man whom he knew had discovered him and given him the first nurturing on the professional stage at Bristol, Nat Brenner. To the veteran director, it was the gift of an opportunity. It was, he told me, 'totally unadulterated bliss'. It was so different a Peter from the one he knew at Bristol. The pose he had struck on the set of *The Lion in Winter* returned. 'He was the father of the company,' said Brenner, a man twenty years O'Toole's senior.

He rehearsed the play in London for a week and then another week in Dublin before the fifteen performances that were given to the Gaiety audiences. It was a ridiculously short run, and should have transferred to London. Several managements expressed interest in it. But there were other thoughts in Peter's mind, other commitments on the horizon. Even so, those who were there say it was the experience of a lifetime. When the play opened, the leading London agent Julian Belfridge told Nat Brenner: 'I think this is the most exciting first night of my life.'

The excitement persisted during the entire run. The Irish Prime Minister, Mr Jack Lynch, had to use influence to get himself a seat. He rang Brenner and told him: 'I understand this is something I should not miss.'

It wasn't. *The Guardian* bemoaning the fact that it wouldn't be seen in London, contented itself with writing about the Dublin triumph. 'Well, they have brought it off,' the paper reported. 'They have shown that Shaw's amusingly tortuous dialogue—so much better read than heard in several recent productions—can if produced with close attention to its rhythms, beguile us with its airy eloquence.

'All in all,' the paper concluded, 'Nat Brenner's production caught the spirit of the comedy with effervescent fun.' That fun persisted so much so that on the final night, with a speech from Eamonn Andrews to send it on its way, the audience spontaneously sang 'Will Ye No Come Back Again', a tribute not often heard in any theatre.

The love affair with Ireland and its theatre continued. Two months after *Man and Superman,* he was starring at the most prestigious of all Dublin theatres, the Abbey, in *Waiting for Godot.* Once more he was playing Vladimir in a way that was quite as polished as it had been at Bristol. Once more he was saying that it was the play that meant more to him than virtually anything else he had ever played. John Barton, the director of another *Godot,* told me: 'I thought he was superb.'

A friend spotted him in his Abbey dressing room waiting to go on stage. 'He was screwed up in a kind of agony,' he reported, 'as if he were in labour. It was the nearest artistic equivalent to giving birth.'

He would dearly have loved to have given birth to a film of *Godot,* but to date it hasn't happened. If he does do it, the camerawork should be done in Ireland. The atmosphere of the country undoubtedly simplifies things for him tremendously, almost as if the little people really have been a help.

Peter himself is convinced that everything about the place is better than it is anywhere else—from a glass of Guinness to the women. He can be totally immersed in a script, but will still have an eye for a pretty girl passing by: 'Have you ever noticed the asses of Irish girls? They're the loveliest in the world.'

He would share the delights of Ireland with his friends. They would go drinking, talk drink and sing Irish songs together—one of them even phoned him from New York to sing a new one he had just discovered. Because drink is such a serious matter, it becomes the subject of bets between members of the O'Toole set. The singing Irishman said it wouldn't be difficult for him to give up the curse of drinking. In fact, he would do it for a whole month. 'You're on,' said Peter. 'I'll be watching you.' He knew his opponent well enough to do the supervising with a stopwatch in hand. The period of abstinence lasted precisely seventeen seconds.

Once, he was asked if he had a drinking problem. 'Drinking is the easiest thing in the world,' he replied. 'Oh, it's true that people like Albert Finney, Richard Burton, Richard Harris and I, do drink. And since we do our drinking in public, we've been known to do a bit of jumping, shrieking and leaping. So what? We're bloody professionals and not one of us has ever been soused on the job.'

Peter couldn't have looked 'the Captain' in the eye again if he had not also sampled the delights of Irish racing. He and his pals went to the world-famous Punchestown steeplechase course, a stretch of racing turf that is about as benign as a minefield. All three friends had backed the winner and were feeling happy enough to compete for buying the booze. But Peter wasn't particularly bothered about celebrating. He had done all that, jumping up and down with excitement when the horse galloped past the winning post. He had won about fifty pounds, and the most important thing was to get to the betting office to collect his winnings.

That and the success of *Godot* seemed to be all that mattered, and the comments of the Irish critics meant that the play had reached his expectations.

If only the tributes to the next O'Toole magnum opus had been quite so enthusiastic. In 1969, *Goodbye Mr Chips* was yet another of those mistakes, even though he again received a nomination for an Academy Award.

The Oscar nomination proved that he had put up a highly creditable performance as the world's favourite old schoolmaster, epitomised for everyone and for ever by Robert Donat. But that was precisely the mistake. The original story was sacred, even though it had not been seen in the theatre for the best part of two generations and had made just a couple of appearances on television. Messing around with it had the unpleasantness of interfering with holy writ.

There were other problems, too. MGM, for whom the movie had been one of the great gems in its history, decided that if the film were to be remade at all, it should be as a musical.

But who should play Chips, the schoolmaster who had become as much a part of Brookfield School as the stone pillars holding up the roof? Laurence Olivier was originally suggested. Then Rex Harrison. Then Richard Burton. All for one reason or another said yes at first and then no. Finally, Peter was mentioned for the part and he said yes. There were similar difficulties with the female star. Julie Andrews was mentioned (she—like Peter—had been shut out of *My Fair Lady,* in which she had so brilliantly created the musical Eliza Doolittle role) but that got no further either. When shooting was about to begin, the part was given to Petula Clark.

The problems with the music were even greater. Composers and lyricists came and went. When the film was all over, John Williams—who orchestrated the new Mr Chips—presented members of the company with an album called:

'MGM Presents The Losers Sing Goodbye Mr Chips . . .' which listed all the film's stars who never were and the directors who had been mentioned before Herbert Ross took over—Vincente Minnelli, Gower Champion et al.

Before Leslie Bricusse was contracted fifty-one songs had been written but the studio decided that they were all too American for such an English story.

It was the studio that was actually responsible for the trouble in the first place. MGM changed hands twice in the years in which the project was discussed and *Chips* ended up looking rather like a car that had been designed under one management and built by another.

None of this was Peter's fault. Nor was it his idea that the story, which in the original spanned the last years of the nineteenth century right up to the thirties, should be brought up to date.

The script was written by Terence Rattigan—but only after there had been so many versions that the producers ran out of colours for the script covers. But Rattigan's script wasn't really brought up-to-date enough. It began in the First World War and ended just after the Second. Chips's wife, so beautifully played in the original by Greer Garson in what was little more than a cameo role (she was on screen for no more than thirty-two minutes), was now portrayed by Petula Clark— who stayed much longer and was killed by a flying bomb instead of the more heartrending (and more romantic?) death suffered by Miss Garson in childbirth. Incidentally, she married Chips only after fighting off the opposition played by one Sian Phillips, a beautiful in-joke if ever there was one.

These were all differences enough to disturb the purists; enough to make it a difficult subject for a musical, although Pet Clark was undoubtedly well cast as the music-hall star Chips marries. (Greer Garson was a maiden lady with more genteel credentials.) The whole project, however, looked like an invitation to bankruptcy.

The matter was made more difficult still by Peter's determination to lay the ghost of Robert Donat. It is easy to see why he wanted to be his own man in the film, but there wasn't the slightest chance in the world that he wouldn't be compared instantly with the original—whatever he managed to change. He would have been better advised to concentrate on the old Chips's kindness and the twinkle in his eye. Instead, Peter wore a pair of spectacles that looked as though they were bought at Woolworth's and a moustache that made him look like a cross between a Nazi gauleiter and Enoch Powell.

There was a great deal of wry humour about him, even though his appearance belied the fact. You couldn't even say that Peter's singing voice helped. As George Baker, who played one of Chips's headmasters in the film, put it: 'You have to admire the courage of a man who believes he can sing. He thought he was doing very well and that he had a very true voice. Well, you have to say that was very brave.' Leslie Bricusse put it more directly. 'He is not exactly renowned for his musicianship.'

After struggling seemingly for days with one particular song, he took off his earphones and told John Williams: 'You know, I think we've got one note from every one of those forty-nine takes.'

George Baker heard the other notes, too. 'You couldn't hear that tape without squirming. But in a way that was just right for Mr Chips. He was not obviously the sort of man who had a good voice.'

O'Toole and Baker together brought some unexpected problems. Both are six feet four inches tall. Both are used to bending the knee to accommodate shorter actors. On *Chips* they did it to help camera angles which were sometimes terribly difficult to light. So first Baker dropped a bit, then it was O'Toole. Herbert Ross looked at this shrinking exercise in sheer amazement. 'If you two fellows keep this up,' he said, 'you'll both be four foot six.

It was another opportunity to see Peter's relationship with his fellow actors at work. Again, he told his director a few times what he thought of him, but for the other actors he was the epitome of consideration. Michael Bryant, who played a German master at Brookfield, had a scene on his own in which he explained why he was leaving for his native country before the outbreak of the war. Peter was merely there to be seen listening to him.

The location used for Brookfield was the beautiful grounds of Sherborne School in Dorset. But all the time Bryant was reciting his speech, an electrical generator could be heard whirring away in the background. Bryant told me that he was so involved with his part that he didn't notice it. But Peter ordered the camera to stop, the sound equipment shut off. 'How the hell do you expect Mr Bryant to work with that generator making all that noise?' And he wouldn't allow the scene to continue until the noise was stopped. It didn't endear him to the technical crew, but Michael Bryant appreciated the gesture tremendously.

The film's producer, Arthur E. Jacobs, appreciated another O'Toole gesture—Peter's contribution to his ashtray collection. Jacobs had been letting it be known that he would appreciate a wholesale ransacking of every hotel and bar within reach of members of the *Mr Chips* company to help swell his collection of souvenirs.

Peter thought this was a fairly easy demand to meet. On the other hand, fairly easy things tend to be uninteresting. But he didn't let his producer down. When he arrived at Sherborne after a weekend in Ireland, he brought the ashtray he had promised, care of Aer Lingus. Only it was a little more than that. The only ashtray he could find on the plane from Dublin was attached to the arm of the seat on which he was sitting. So he broke off the arm and gave that to Jacobs when he arrived on the set.

Some of the location work was done among the ruins of Pompeii, which Peter found to be just as exciting as the job of playing 'Mr Cheeps'—as the locals called it. The very fact that he was working in Italy at all, after all the things he had said about the paparazzi, was remarkable in itself. But he protected himself. Ex-boxing champ, Dave Crowley, who owned a drinking establishment called Dave's Dive was with him again, prepared to press his fists between any difficult photographers who managed to get on to the set.

But most of the filming took place in Dorset. Peter and Sian took a cottage near Sherborne and enjoyed the nearest thing to a holiday either had had for years. He became a close friend of Robert Powell, the Sherborne Headmaster, who was acting as technical adviser on the movie, and spent a great deal of time with him discussing Romanesque architecture. From Powell, he got to know not a little about schoolmasters. 'Chips,' he declared, 'was a pretty dreadful teacher.'

Quite early on, people were anxious to know why he made the film. 'The only thing that caused me to read it was the fact that the script was by Terry Rattigan,' he explained after saying that the idea of a musical *Chips* filled him with horror. But his knowledge of literature was enough to make him think that it might not be so bad. 'Terry isn't an oilpainter so much as a line drawer and he's written a beautiful script for the film, elegant down to the last detail.

'It's not the sort of screen musical either where everything stops for five minutes while some bloke yells the place down.'

It was not a film in which heavy drinking was called for. Peter's concession towards fitting into the shoes of the abstemious Mr Chipping was to make do with light ale.

Another difference was that he spent very little time socialising with his leading lady. Everynight Petula Clark used to fly to France, where she had her home, so as not to infringe the regulations which would make her liable for British income tax.

The film didn't take enough money to make tax the main problem. But when it had its world premiere in New York, it was clear that O'Toole's performance had again outmatched the actual film. Writing in the *New York Times,* Vincent Canby said that the film's single redeeming feature was Peter himself. 'If it survived, it was because of the "restrained affectingly comic performance of Peter O'Toole in the title role".'

148

The London *Daily Mirror's* Dick Richards said: 'Peter O'Toole gives a most impressive performance—quiet, subtle. But he isn't Mr Chips. Passed over for the headmastership of Brookfield School, he humbly accepts the disappointment. O'Toole's Mr Chips would, I think, have said: "To hell with them," and moved to fresh pastures . . . The real trouble, I think, is that whenever one is getting absorbed in the gentle story, there's a feeling that every line of dialogue is probably a cue for Pet Clark or Peter O'Toole to sing an indifferent song. They usually do.'

Peter had his own ideas about the next song he wanted to sing. He was going to film the play that had represented his first triumph at Stratford, *The Merchant of Venice*. Jules Buck liked the idea. It was the perfect next production for Keep Films. MGM thought so, too. But then Peter's Shylock was involved in just the same problems that had caused so much trouble for *Mr Chips*. The men who said yes to the film had gone, replaced by others who thought that the whole notion of *The Merchant* was enough to spark off a new outbreak of anti-Semitism.

Had the film been made, it might have proved a good augury for the new decade. As it was, the seventies and the year that followed them were going to prove the most difficult in his life.

Eleven

JULES BUCK KNEW his business partner. 'It depends what sort of mood he's in,' he said. 'If it's Peter's Yorkshire mood then it'll be all right. He's sensible and makes all the right decisions. But if he's in his Irish mood, duck.'

The seventies was going to be the decade for ducking; when the Irishman in O'Toole took over, leaving the fellow from Leeds all too few opportunities to make the right decisions, although there were a couple of occasions when reason did prevail.

Murphy's War was not one, although it was generally accepted that Peter was a great deal better than the movie, a situation that was not at all novel. Peter was seen at his untidiest, sweatiest, dirtiest, playing the part of a sailor in Venezuela. Mind you, considering some of the choice expressions he used to describe the Orinoco River, that was perhaps not all that difficult. Indeed, he was earning $250,000 for the privilege.

Murphy was a sailor who had been torpedoed by a U-boat. Now, like a demented Captain Ahab searching for the whale in *Moby Dick,* he was determined to get the submarine even, if it meant bombing it from a home-made aeroplane.

But the sailor getting himself torpedoed sometimes seemed as nothing compared with all the problems of filming up the Orinoco. 'It was a somewhat harrowing experience,' the director Peter Yates, told me. 'Most of it geographical. But Peter was extraordinary and his support was magnificent.'

One of the reasons for that support—and again contrary to what both of them had been saying—was that Sian was in the film playing a pacifist doctor. 'He was desperately anxious that it should go right for her.' But there were problems.

Peter himself said that half the difficulty was simply the title. *Murphy's War* sounded too much like Murphy's Law, which, in filmmaking parlance, means simply that anything that can go wrong will. And it did. Another interpretation of Murphy's Law is that nothing is ever as simple as it looks and everything takes longer than you expect.

When Peter looked out of one of the portholes of the Belfast-to-Liverpool ferry that had been converted to accommodate the film crew, he said just one word—'Buckets'. That meant it was raining, when it shouldn't have been. Nor should the boat have gone aground. Nor should they have been satisfied with five minutes' filming on a good day. But things were going so badly that Peter stopped writing in the journal he sometimes keeps while on location. It made too depressing writing, let alone reading.

The crew were mostly Irish, which Peter found quite useful. The sound of their voices turned out to be a fairly reliable tuning-fork for the Dublin accent he was using for the part.

Nevertheless, the crew were not quite what he was originally hoping for. As with all his work, he began preparations for *Murphy's War* in every detail. For him, that included trying to learn the language. Since the movie was being shot in Venezuela, this meant learning Spanish. He thought there would be a great number of Venezuelans to talk to. There weren't. As Peter Yates said: 'Poor Peter had learned a language and yet was up the creek with an English-speaking crew in a Spanish-speaking country making a British film with American money.'

Most of the film people stayed in the town of Port Odaz—grandly spoken of as the 'Cleveland of Venezuela'. But in order to give Sian a rest, the O'Tooles slept on their boat. He thought it was the best way of seeing something of the

151

countryside, too. Whenever he could, he borrowed the crew's helicopter to take him over the surrounding area. 'He just didn't want to think he was wasting the opportunity of being in a new country,' said Yates. 'He wanted to feel that he had gone over the same territory as Sir Walter Raleigh.'

He asked a group of Indians to take him up into uncharted territory. They said no. He asked again. Still no. But eventually he managed to cajole a couple of men to go with him deep into the jungle—where the natives would sniff a certain tree root which made them high enough to indulge in their cannibal activities. Peter got out only when he realised that the pigmy-sized natives were skilled at using bows and arrows that he couldn't even lift.

Peter has never been a hypochondriac, but on this trip he took so many medicines, pills and other potions with him that the unit doctor said he was a walking apothecary.

Sian's role off the camera was even more effective. When, in the interests of the movie, he had too much to drink, she was on hand to put her arms around him and take him to a quiet corner.

Some of the battle scenes were done in Malta. And for these, Peter went back to his early filming habits and performed his own stunts—including swimming in an oil-filled sea with explosions going on all around him. They were his first since *Lawrence* when, after his assortment of resultant injuries, he said he would never do any stunts again. But now, he thought, why not? The man who had noticed the onset of middle age now felt young.

In Venezuela, he even learned to fly a seaplane himself. 'If you want to see an expression of pure terror,' he said, 'look at me in that plane.'

His only disagreement with the director was when his French co-star Phillipe Noiret was taken ill and sent to hospital. Yates didn't go to see him and Peter wanted to know why. 'We actors do all this work and get no appreciation,' said O'Toole angrily.

'Of course, Peter was quite right. I'd been working and hadn't found the time. But I should have done.'

152

It was an expensive film to make and not just because of the star salaries and the travelling involved. The U-boat was hired from the Venezuelan navy, and the boat it sank was bought for twenty thousand dollars.

When the picture was finally wrapped up, not many voices of regret could be heard. Michael Deeley, the producer, said that Peter had been a 'saint'. He could have given them trouble, but he was kindness and co-operation itself. Again the critics praised O'Toole's performance but said that the movie itself was unworthy of him.

The New York *Daily News* was even less charitable. It wrote of a picture which 'offers no challenge to his acting ability, but is only a test of his physical endurance; a sluggish action spectacle'.

Not many writers were yet asking why he was apparently wasting that talent called Peter O'Toole. If they had, he might have asked himself. He professed not to worry. He said that he woke up each morning grateful that he had survived another night, and that covered everything he ever did. Not quite. He was also a pessimist, the kind who believes that in front of every silver lining is a black cloud. That was probably why in the best spirit of 'the Captain', he constantly hedged his bets. If there was money to be made, he would do what the chequebook dictated. Lord Olivier once explained that the reason he made so many indifferent pictures in his later life was to 'put something in the larder'. That was Peter's sentiment precisely. What he should have realised was that he was slowly driving his career into limbo.

The films were subsidising the luxury of doing 'real' acting on the live stage. There could have been better films to make, even more commercial plays to do in the West End. And yet he welcomed opportunities to play uncommercial roles in theatres outside London which other stars in his bracket would have regarded as positively beneath them.

In 1971, he scored a triumph in another presentation of *Waiting for Godot* which the *Daily Telegraph* described as 'very Irish'—even though it was being presented at the Nottingham Playhouse.

It was a time when he got himself into more trouble than he could have anticipated. While in the city he agreed to draw a raffle. The winner couldn't be found, so he tried again and gave the one hundred pound prize to someone else. Then the original winner came to claim the prize. He gave her instead the proceeds of his bet on a race that day. 'What a lovely man,' said the woman—who had previously said some very unlovely things about him.

The fact that Fleet Street thought it important enough to make the trip northwards to review *Waiting for Godot* gives further indication of the value that a Peter O'Toole performance still represented. In *The Times,* Irving Wardle wrote that O'Toole 'forces his voice into bursts of excitement and flaps round the stage as a scarecrow dandy'. The play was an achievement, he wrote.

Wardle also stressed the way Peter was able to relate to the other tramp in the piece played by Donald McCann. Peter himself discussed this. He said it was a similar sort of relationship to the one he had built up with Richard Burton in *Becket.* 'Yes,' he said, 'every man needs a husband.'

As a husband himself, Peter didn't really seem to be in need of much. He wasn't the kind of man who spent a lot of time on sport, although he said he played a vicious game of croquet. He stayed in evenings fairly often—with a box of table-tennis balls by his side which he could use for throwing at the television screen when something offended his sense of dramatic taste. This was a compromise enforced by Sian; after he had thrown a portable television through the screen of the family's big TV set.

When the O'Tooles could get away, they would go to Venice; always in the wintertime, when it rained and when there were no other tourists, collecting more archaeological specimens.

His home was filling up with these now, and with his other collecting passion, Japanese Noh masks. He would soon have another home to fill with them, too. He and Sian were having one built in Connemara, high on the hill at Clifden, a structure created from local stone and which faced the sea.

For all his barnstorming reputation, Peter constantly gave indications of his other self; the considerate, affectionate, deeply sensitive person—the one who, on a trip to Scotland, would weep at the fate of ninety percent of the salmon which fail to make the swim upstream and die in the process; the man who could take his children out to the Clifden coast and find himself explaining about the dangers of the sea as though describing the need to be careful when getting on a bus. They sat on a rock and Peter told them about the dangers of tides and to be very careful walking along the rocks.

Was he more mellow? He didn't think he was. 'I still have this self-destructive streak,' he told writer Peter Evans. 'There is nothing like a few bob to cure Socialism, is there? I have a house and children. I'm not the big bad wolf about to huff and puff and blow the house down.'

'All experience, in my experience, corrupts. You learn too many tricks. Tell me any experience that you've had that enobles you. Go on!' It wouldn't have mattered if any had been offered. Peter wouldn't have believed him. At least, he wouldn't have said that he did. His greatest strength—and his weakness, too—was being very firmly set in his views. It carried him to his finest triumphs and his worst failures.

If there had been disappointments over some of his films, everyone got exactly what they expected from *Under Milk Wood,* the 1977 film of Dylan Thomas's play, in which Peter played the blind Captain Cat. A labour of love if ever there had been one, it was a marriage of the non-commercial theatre which O'Toole loved, with the films, which he only allowed himself to do for the sake of cash. This time there was no cash, but it was a chance to re-do Dylan Thomas's classic—and to work with Richard Burton once more. Not just Burton, either, but Elizabeth Taylor thrown in for good measure as Rosie Probert, the girl of his dreams. To keep an eye on things, Sian agreed, yet again, to work with Peter as the fastidious Mrs Ogmore Pritchard.

In spite of this illustrious line-up, Leslie Halliwell commented: 'Attractive but vaguely unsatisfactory screen rendering of an essentially theatrical event. Everything is much too literal—a real place instead of a fantasy.'

The Ruling Class in 1971 was very different. It was a picture that achieved that supreme accolade in controversy—the first to do so for Peter since *Lawrence of Arabia*—correspondence in *The Times*.

Churchmen and churchgoers decided that both the star and the movie itself were blasphemous. Perhaps not an unreasonable sentiment since Peter appeared in the film as a long-haired eccentric who imagines himself as The Holy Trinity All In One—to be called, he demands, by any of the nine billion names of God. He also manages to get himself quite effectively crucified.

After an extract had been featured on BBC television, Miss Catherine Bramwell Booth, descendant of the founder of the Salvation Army, wrote to *The Times*: 'Is there, Sir, no power in all the land, able to prevent the intrusion into any programme of such a beastly travesty of Him Whom I Hold Most Holy?'

Of course, the man, one Jack Gurney, 14th Earl of Gurney, is plainly mad—he even commits murder—and Peter was always very good playing eccentrics. Watching how he darts from place to place, it is easy to see where he got his way with director, Peter Medak. 'I had to accept that he would,' Medak told me. 'When you get a good actor, one has to accept that personalities will clash.' And clash they did—'as inevitably they do when you have to deal with strong-minded people'.

Medak wanted the scene at the end of the film, where Peter kills Coral Browne, to dissolve in a very complicated shot filmed through a corridor. 'He said it made him look as if he were in two places at the same time. It wouldn't have been

156

like that because there would have been tricks in cutting. In the end we compromised—and did it in a way completely different from the manner in which either of us had suggested it.

'But it was a wonderful experience and I loved doing the movie. I had been trying to set it up for two years.'

One critic described it is an 'irritating and unsatisfying film that is worth being unsatisfied by'. It was notable in that it was the first O'Toole film in which there were critics who said he was upstaged by supporting players—in this case, Arthur Lowe and Alastair Sim.

Peter himself was the first to appreciate their talents. He paid Michael Bryant, who was also in the film, the biggest compliment of all. He wept. 'Peter, what's the matter?' asked Bryant, extremely disturbed to see his colleague in a state usually seen only when tragedy is afoot—or when salmon don't manage the high jump. 'I just love it! Love it!' Peter explained. 'Nothing moves me like great acting.'

He said he himself was pleased to make the story because he was appalled at all the violence and sex in films. 'I'm not a prude,' he told David Lewin. 'But I think sex is to be enjoyed.'

By all accounts, Peter enjoyed making the film, and so did the people working with him. James Villiers was in it, too, and they shared a house together. It was the scene of a number of uproarious parties—including one when Peter bet his old friend that he couldn't drink a concoction of every drink in the house. Villiers said he could—at which Peter poured into a long sundae-type glass a mixture of whisky, brandy, rum, Drambuie and every other alcoholic liquid in the building. 'Of course, I couldn't. But we also bet everyone else in the house. The result was that we raised about £500 for charity.' And the drink? 'It was terrible, absolutely undrinkable.'

The fact that *The Ruling Class* seemed to be enjoyed by most of the critics, Peter said, was 'good for the tissues', although there had been editing disputes with United Artists.

And on the whole, they did enjoy his cavorting around the set, expecting the genuflections granted to God one moment, doing an elaborate country dance with Carolyn Seymour the next, followed by cutting people up like Jack the Ripper.

Someone quite seriously asked him at this time if he would like to play in a new version of *Dr Jekyll and Mr Hyde.* He said that Dr Jekyll bored him tremendously. But Mr Hyde was another matter entirely. That excited him. He was, of course, very similar to Jack Gurney.

'Madness was never my idea of a joke,' wrote Cecil Wilson in the London *Daily Mail,* reviewing *The Ruling Class,* 'but there are disarming shafts of logic in the lunacy and Peter O'Toole, wild-eyed and nobly spoken, sweeps titanically through a delirium of slapstick, melodrama, song and dance.'

When *The Ruling Class* had its American premiere, United Artists provided a galaxy of 'belted earls', as they rather ungallantly described them, to be snapped by cameramen.

The *New York Times*, which always takes things more seriously, said in its piece by John Simon: 'There is Peter O'Toole, as mercurial as he is incisive, a Jack who does the most outrageous things with a bemusedly introspective air, who gives absurd romantic-heroic stature and makes crude farce so dainty and elegant that the film acquires another dimension by his mere presence.'

The picture was Britain's principal entry for the 1971 Cannes Film Festival. Some people complained that it was too long by about half an hour. 'So is the week,' said Peter.

Unfortunately, for Keep Films—and for Jules Buck and the ailing Jack Hawkins who jointly acted as producers—the takings for the film failed totally to match up to the reaction of the critics.

It turned out to be one of the reasons for the eventual break up in the partnership between Buck and O'Toole. Peter has always made great play of having no head for business and said that he formed Keep Films as much to keep out the accountants as to keep the profits. He would have been much wiser to leave all the business headaches to United Artists. Instead, some time later, he decided to buy up the distribution rights to the film. He was not happy with what the Hollywood company had done with what he regarded as a highly commercial property. The result was that he lost nearly a million pounds. Once more, he was all but broke. But he had ways of improving that situation, one of which was to make another musical.

Man of La Mancha was a huge off-Broadway success, playing in a theatre in Washington Square that nightly did more business than any of the playhouses on Broadway. In London, this musical version of the story of Don Quixote and Sancho Panza had a much less enthusiastic following, although the principal song 'The Impossible Dream' got whistled and sung everywhere.

United Artists clearly hoped that making a film version of the play in 1972 would bring in all those who stayed away from the stage musical—as well as those who had enjoyed it in New York. If they didn't go for Peter O'Toole—and the reckoning was that they would—then Sophia Loren, showing more of her ample bosom in a ragged, tight-fitting dress than even her normally generous self usually allowed, surely would.

Peter's principles were torn to shreds by agreeing to make the movie. It was filmed in Rome, yet the financial compensation was plainly worth the risk. But there were difficulties. For one thing, he had to agree to have early nights. As he said at the time: 'The man who invented mornings was no Christian. I prefer to go straight into the afternoon.'

Peter took singing lessons to improve on his performance in *Mr Chips* and sounded the better for it, but the movie was no hit.

It cost eleven million dollars—because, Peter alleged, it wasn't made by professionals but by businessmen, 'the cornflakes men'—and they're only in it for the girls'.

'You used to join amateur dramatics to get at the crackling,' he said at the time. 'These men buy up studios to achieve the same end. You see them flying around in their private jets with birds we used to hide under the table fifteen years ago. It's insane. Crackling should be an added bonus, not an end in itself.'

That was just a little contempt to heap on his general feelings about the way *Man of La Mancha* had been handled. He was enthusiastic from the beginning because he liked the way Peter Granville, the director, and writer John Hopkins were going to go back to the original story by Cervantes. That, however, was not the way United Artists saw it at all. They had spent a lot of money buying the rights to the stage play and were not going to be satisfied with simply a story that was in the public domain. So director and writer were sacked. Little love was clearly lost between the new director, Arthur Hiller—whom Peter insisted on calling 'Little Arthur'—and the star.

O'Toole clanked away in his armour—which was actually made of plastic; the noises were added afterwards—taking no more notice of Hiller than he had to. Sophia Loren, apparently, felt much the same way.

For all that, it was another distinctly O'Toole performance. There was a feeling similar to the one that came with watching *Lawrence,* that the original character must have looked precisely like Peter. As you watched the long, bent, spindly frame of Quixote in the film, with his pointed beard and piercing eyes, it was difficult to imagine that Cervantes had not been gifted with a kind of uncanny vision into the future and seen Peter as his crazy knight errant all the time.

The reaction of the press was familiar, too. In the London *Sunday Telegraph,* Margaret Hinxman wrote: '. . . Without much enthusiasm, I found myself dreaming the impossible dream, bearing that unbearable sorrow and gazing into a nobler future as if I were on the payroll of *Man of La Mancha* . . . Peter O'Toole is splendid.' There were similar bouquets on the other side of the Atlantic. In California, the *Hollywood Reporter* said he was brilliant. It was a 'rich, totally committed performance'.

When it was all over, Peter confessed he was absolutely exhausted. 'These days,' he said 'you not only have to make films. You have to flog them, too.' He was tired, also, of having to flog himself, so he was taking a long, long holiday.

Twelve

FOR EIGHTEEN MONTHS, Peter O'Toole stayed out of the public's attention. For most of the time he was in Ireland, digging ditches for the sewerage of his new house in Clifden, advising the architects, and . . . just thinking.

The scripts tumbled through the letterbox of the house in Hampstead and when he was there, he read them and decided that they didn't interest him much. Sian was around a lot of the time, appearing in films and television plays on her own. She was free to do what she liked. 'There's a ring around her finger, not her nose,' said Peter.

He had decided he was entitled to the sabbatical other people plan but never get round to having. He had finished *La Mancha* thinner than he began it. So thin, in fact, that Sian had got to calling him The Bone. His face was gaunt and his stomach hurt. Like a quarterly bill from the gas and electricity authorities, his doctors periodically told him to lay off the booze, but he took no more notice now than he had ever done before. And there were still troubles with his eyes; the bits still had to be scraped away at regular intervals.

He thought of broadening his education. He read a lot, went on with his collecting, but he always felt that something was missing—inevitable for anyone who had left school at fourteen. With his friend, Professor Moelwyn Merchant, he discussed a stay at Exeter University, with a view to studying Shakespeare in greater depth. When he thought about his career, it continued to be negatively. He

162

didn't want the West End. He didn't want Hollywood any more now than he ever had before, but neither did he want the British film industry.

What did appeal, however, was a call from Bristol. Would he consider going back for a short season? Consider? It was what he wanted more than anything else.

In 1973, Val May was trying to find a way of bringing the people back to the Theatre Royal, that 'jewel box' which Peter had loved so much. The theatre itself was as it was. But it was now encased in a fine modern complex—a superb foyer, restaurants, offices, waiting areas. 'It was so good that the people were being frightened of going back,' said May. 'We were worried.'

It was Nat Brenner, now running the Old Vic's school, who suggested that he might be able to persuade Peter O'Toole to come. If he would, the change could be tremendous. The public would be sure to follow.

'Do you think he would?' May asked. 'I think he just might,' said Brenner, who still knew his old pupil. Peter needed little persuasion.

Suddenly, there was an opportunity to go back to his happiest days. The greyhound was racing again—more anxious than ever to feel his feet on the King Street cobblestones. As far as the theatre was concerned, it was an investment far and beyond Bristol itself. For now, with the opening of new motorways, it was less than two and a half hours away from London. So the theatre would no longer be depending on local audiences.

Brenner wanted Peter to do three plays—not even O'Toole could be excused the rigours of repertory, for that was part of the appeal of Bristol. They asked him to think about Chekhov's *Uncle Vanya, The Apple Cart* by Shaw and the Ben Travers farce *Plunder*.

May would direct the first, David Phethean the second, and Brenner the last. There was no question of his being paid for the plays. What, after all, could Bristol pay him? Nothing to compare with his normal salaries, and if he didn't do live theatre for cash, why should he deplete the Old Vic's finances? They would feel the pinch much more than he would benefit from it.

The theatre was asked to find him a home, and eventually, a gracious house was found in a square at Clifton. There, Peter comfortably ensconsed himself for the three months his stay at Bristol lasted. He settled down to work like a student at his first class. It felt new and exciting.

'Oh, he was in magnificent form,' Nat Brenner recalls. 'Artistically, he was in marvellous nick and he brought the people back again. They had got out of the habit of going to the Old Vic.'

He took his work as seriously as if he had been paid a million dollars for a part that would be seen by theatre critics all over the world. This was no easy option for him; every matinée was a first night. He advised on the company, too. Once more, Nigel Stock was with him in each of the plays. So was Edward Hardwicke and Judy Parfitt. Peter O'Toole wanted the *Uncle Vanya* that the people of Bristol would see to be the definitive performance. There were several translations of the play and he sought them all before deciding which one he was going to use. There had also been a Russian film of the play. That, he decided, might give him the feel of the original, even if he couldn't understand the dialogue. He knew what was being said in what circumstances and that would have to be enough. So he rang the Soviet Embassy in London and arranged to see the movie for himself.

The homework proved worthwhile. 'What amazed me,' said Val May, 'was how different this Peter O'Toole was from the one I had first met in 1966. He was pleasant and brilliant. I was astonished when we had our first reading of the play that he knew Vanya's lines completely by heart. The only thing was he had learned a different version from the one I had.' It was, needless to say, O'Toole's that was adopted.

His view of the first reading set the trend for what would follow. 'Every rehearsal was exciting,' said May. 'Co-operative in every way.' But perhaps a little disconcerting. There is one scene in the play when a professor says he is going to sell Vanya's land. The main character then has to show his anger at this treachery. O'Toole didn't just get angry. 'He went wild,' said Val May. 'In fact, I thought he had gone crazy. He threw furniture around at this rehearsal and then started to physically attack people. I was terrified.' Then, quite suddenly, he stopped.

'I just did it to show the intensity of this man's feelings,' Peter explained as though saying why he had just bought a new car.

'The performance he gave as Vanya was captivating,' said Brenner. 'He was giving a personal appearance instead of merely appearing in a play.' On the first night, in October 1973, he received a standing ovation—and there was one practically every night afterwards. At the first night party on the stage, he danced with the girls from the box office.

It wasn't the only thing that happened on that stage without the general public knowing. There was, for instance, the night that Peter shot Nigel Stock—in just the scene that had caused all the commotion in rehearsal.

Stock, playing the professor, was supposed to be shot before the curtain came down. Every night, Peter fired the gun with his right hand, holding it upwards. Every night, that is, except the one when he held the pistol in his left hand and pointed it downwards. Peter was about a foot and a half away from his intended victim when he misdirected the shot. 'I suddenly felt a sensation in my right calf much as though I had been hit by someone using an iron bar,' Stock told me. 'I fell into a chair and couldn't get up. The curtain came down and everyone expected me to move away—but I couldn't.'

Totally unpredictably, the blank cartridge had shot into Stock's leg instead of falling away. He spent the rest of the run of the play sitting down or using a stick.

The matter was hushed up at the time and until now, no one has ever mentioned it. 'It hurt quite a bit, I can tell you,' said Nigel Stock. 'But no one was more upset than Peter.

He couldn't understand how it had happened. He was absolutely shattered.'

The papers may not have known about the shooting, but they loved the play just the same. David Foot wrote in *The Guardian:* 'Peter O'Toole shuffles down the steps into a garden. His mouth sags in geriatric despair. His red-rimmed eyes are filled with Chekhovian pain. He is old before his time. It is an entrance worth waiting fifteen years for.'

They said the same sort of thing about the other plays in the series, too. About *Plunder,* Eric Shorter in the *Daily Telegraph* had a few reservations. He wrote: 'Mr O'Toole gangles and dithers nicely as the silly ass who gets caught up in the crookery but asinuity is not really in his line.'

But Mr Shorter was in no doubt about the success of the season as a whole and when he reviewed *The Apple Cart,* he said that 'O'Toole's presence at the Theatre Royal has not only put the company on its feet by ensuring full houses throughout the season. It has also drawn first-rate players in support.'

Val May had no doubt about what Peter contributed to the Old Vic in the city. 'He saved our bacon. We never looked back after that. I must say that I had never really thought of him in that context, but when I saw him at Bristol in 1973, I knew I was watching a genius'.

'He should have taken all three of those plays to London. His *Plunder* was better than the one the National did.' But it was only so after Peter had satisfied himself that it would be. When he discovered that the nonogenarian Ben Travers was still alive, he travelled to the capital to meet him to discuss the play.

'I think he drew strength from the plays,' said Brenner. And the plays benefited from him.

One of the greatest O'Toole achievements while in Bristol was a matinée performance given before an invited audience of local dignitaries and theatre lovers. He gave a virtuoso solo reading of a four-hour story about soldiers who turn into cannibals. He stood on a stage with just a lectern, a couple of chairs and a glass of water. And for four hours he mesmerised his audience. 'It was a wonderful moment,' recalled Val May.

But he wasn't well. He was suffering from stomach pains which grew ever more excruciating. He was much thinner and his face was grey, he tried to stifle the pain with pills, but they weren't very effective. It was a condition he tried to keep to himself. 'He was making about fifteen deals with film companies,' said Val May, 'and I think he was worried about his insurance prospects. But I think he was very, very brave.'

But he mixed with the other players and with everyone else in the company, too. He was the most popular man to have played in the theatre for years. Each night, he would pop into the box office to ask about business. If he felt like having a drink in the city, he would go down the street, wearing a long raincoat, a hat over his eyes and dark glasses—'looking.' as one employee of the theatre told me, 'just like Peter O'Toole.'

He was also extremely sociable and generous. He played host at parties—without, this time, any unpleasantness. After the final performance, he gave one party at his house at which the drink flowed so prodigiously that practically nobody was able to do any work the next day—or take part in the theatre's Christmas party.

There were now other things for him to do. When the idea came up for a film in Mexico to be based on the Robinson Crusoe story, it seemed a good idea. *Man Friday,* made in 1975, was virtually a duet between Peter and the black actor Richard Rowntree. It concentrated on the bond between the two men and was hailed at the time as the perfect study in race relations. It wasn't a perfect film but its director, Jack Gold, was thrilled at being chosen for the job by Peter.

There were the usual problems and a few more. 'The biggest problem was the weather,' Jack Gold told me. Shooting had been scheduled for Puerto Vallarta, which John Huston had discovered before it became a famous tourist resort—a sort of Mexican Hollywood. Every morning, the crew would set out for the location in bright sunlight. By the

167

time they got there, a heavy black cloud had descended. Nevertheless, the impression of a hot desert island was still created out of this Mexican mainland town. 'He suggested a number of ideas,' said Gold. 'Only a fool would fail to accept that sort of advice. He helped get the film off the ground.'

It was a happy time for Peter and a formative one. Sian was at home—and Peter had fallen in love with a Mexican waitress. Her name was Malinche Verdugo, who wanted to become an actress. The relationship would develop, but it didn't prevent him from having fun with other people on the set. He taught Richard Rowntree how to play English football. He used his Spanish to laugh with the other Mexicans on the set and, with impersonations of Max Miller and Sid Field, introduced them to English music hall.

Mexico, largely through Malinche, stayed in the O'Toole psyche. He made his next film, *Foxtrot,* with Charlotte Rampling there, too, in 1975. The film never amounted to anything and wasn't even released in Britain. *Variety* said of it: '*Foxtrot* is a chic, stylish but ultimately hollow Peter O'Toole starrer made in Mexico about a decadent Roumanian aristocrat retreating to a desert island with wife Charlotte Rampling on the eve of World War Two . . . it often lapses from wild irony into cornball melodrama . . .'

There were obviously strains in the marriage. Peter knew he was spending too much time away from Sian, but not even their closest friends thought there was anything wrong. They still went out to dinner parties together. When friends called, they were still their old, happy selves. Or so it seemed.

They did, however, make great play of the fact that they sincerely believed in the need for independence. And that went for their daughters, too. Kate and Pat had their own flat in the house at Heath Street and to listen to their parents, they lived a totally separate—and the way they saw it—middle-aged life. When they had problems it was Peter to whom they would go. 'He's a marvellous father,' Sian told friends, and she meant it. It was perfectly true. The only blot in their perfect relationship was Peter's inordinate curiosity. He could never resist opening their mail.

Sian loved Peter quite as much as he loved her—and, no matter what had happened, there was no doubt that he still adored her. When asked if she was jealous, she said that if another woman did come on the scene, she was sure there would be a good reason for it. But she said she wasn't frightened of it happening, because Peter was 'such a loner'.

Sian was no longer quoted as saying, 'We are Peter's refuge, his fortress, his castle', but there were times when it looked like it.

They avoided shouting at each other. At least Sian never shouted at Peter—although Peter would find excuses to shout at everyone. He continued to buy her antique jewellery, because diamonds always seemed like glass to her, and sometimes they would work together in the garden at Hampstead growing their own vegetables. If that seemed like a cosy domestic arrangement, there was another. Sian's aged mother lived with them, too.

For the moment his ill health seemed to be in check and there was little to show that he had any problems at all. He had started working on another picture. Neither *Man Friday* nor *Foxtrot* had worked very well. 'It wasn't very good, was it?' asked Peter when discussing the Charlotte Rampling picture. 'There's been an awful dearth of good material.' He was concerned about his age again, and as he said, 'Don't forget, the forties are the forties. They affect men as much as women.'

But he still kept trying. He made a film in Israel about PLO terrorists, called *Rosebud*—it had nothing to do with the famous last line in *Citizen Kane*—and came into collision a couple of times with the Israeli police who forced down his light aircraft. And there was another fracas, too. This time in Paris—where some other work for the film was being done. Writer Kenneth Tynan had decided that it was time for an O'Toole leg pull. He sent a note to the studio to say that since

169

Peter was a very bad Irishman who had not done enough to help the IRA—the terrorists would now get him. To add fuel to the allegations of the anonymous letter writer, he said that an explosive device would before long be blowing up on the set.

That was not the kind of letter anyone likes receiving. To arrive in the middle of the shooting of a film about the PLO and Middle East terrorism, it is likely to cause considerable panic—which is precisely what did happen. The set was ransacked, but no bomb was found. But Peter did discover the identity of the letter's writer.

Accompanied by a posse of Irish crewmen (their nationality being nothing more than a coincidence) the O'Toole fists banged on the door of Tynan's Paris office and he and his friends forced their way into the room where the writer was for the moment laughing uproariously. He didn't stay laughing for very long.

The language was colourful and fists flew—a couple of them into Tynan's groin. 'I was well and truly beaten up,' said a somewhat chastened Tynan afterwards.

Rosebud got a similar reaction. 'Confused, rambling and almost totally lacking in suspense,' said Arthur Thirkell in the London *Daily Mirror*. The *Daily Mail* said, 'the drama is curiously flat, unmotivated. And I think O'Toole could have acted a little more as if he meant it.'

They hadn't said that about Peter's acting before, but then he only took the role in the first place because his sabbatical and the season at Bristol still had to be financed.

He was plainly worried about himself. He confessed once that there were times when we woke up not knowing who he was. 'And when I found out, I wasn't too pleased about it.' The second sentence was intended as light relief, but he inwardly meant it. And the heart of the matter wasn't funny at all. 'I've lost edge and appetite for the thing I love most—which is acting.'

Interviewers tended to worry about their safety in his presence. They were anxious about the stares he gave them, but he was usually kind, generous and charming. 'I won't answer questions, or give interviews,' he told one obviously upset journalist. 'But you can talk to me. No questions because that'll be an interview.' They then proceeded to have a highly amusing and productive two-way chat.

When the BBC asked him to talk to them, he seemed churlish. 'Look,' one of the men from the Corporation told him, 'we don't have to do this interview you know.'

'In that case,' said Peter, 'I suggest you bugger off.'

When he didn't want to work, he was content to watch Sian's career blossom. She had been brilliant in a series about the British suffragette leader, Mrs Pankhurst, and there was to be a notable success for her in a new BBC television project, *I, Claudius,* which would focus the attention of the nation on Ancient Rome. Peter also advised on some of the work she did—and commented on a few of the things said about her. Someone had the cheek to suggest that she was too aristocratic to appear as Beth Morgan in *How Green Was My Valley*.

'Too aristocratic!' he steamed, 'She's a bloody peasant! She's from a farm in Gwaun-cae-Gurwen. You can't get more peasant than that. You should see her when I'm getting the scorching tongue. Ah, but every man should have his Sian.' The trouble was that he could no longer be sure that he did have his own Sian.

Thirteen

EARLY IN 1975, problems descended on Peter like a series of punches in a pub brawl. As he later told writer David Lewin, it was as though his 'bookie's double' had gone down.

He finally accepted his doctor's recommendation that if he continued to drink, he would die. But that wasn't enough. The abdominal pains became so much worse that he was rushed from the house in Heath Street to the Royal Free Hospital close by. It specialises in liver and kidney complaints.

Within hours of his arrival there, an exploratory operation was carried out. But there was no easy answer forthcoming. No evidence of cancer or of a dozen other possible serious illnesses. However, it was clear that Peter *was* very severely ill. He was fed pure water by tube into his stomach and wasn't allowed any solid food. The hospital placed him in a side ward and he was registered as a National Health Service patient.

He arrived at the hospital with a full growth of beard. One of the first things his nurses did was to start to shave it off. 'Hey, don't do that,' he pleaded in a voice so weak it would never have been picked up by a boom microphone. 'I need it.'

He was to have worn it in his first television spectacular for years, playing Judas in the ATV special on the life of Christ. That was lost with a great part of the O'Toole entrails. Eventually, surgeons diagnosed panchriatitis, a condition that is frequently fatal. If it had not been spotted at just that

172

time—and if the surgeons had not dealt with the matter as skilfully as they had—it would have been a killer for Peter, too.

There wasn't just one operation. The condition was so critical—as he put it 'several yards of interior plumbing' had to be removed—that it was done in stages. It was a depressing time for him. There were days when he tried in vain to pull out the various tubes attached to his anatomy, but was restrained by the nurses.

No one told Peter he was likely to die, but he was too intelligent not to appreciate that there was something very critically wrong with him. What worried him most were the jolly looks on the faces of the people who came to visit him with their flowers and bunches of grapes. They were decidedly too funny, trying just that little bit too hard to cheer him up. What none of them knew at the time was that he had considerable need for cheering up—and not just because of his health.

Sian had decided to leave him. He was so wrapped up in his own career and there were so many stories about other women in his life that she had had enough. When he was first taken to the hospital, she came to see him regularly. Then, when he was beginning to get better, she just stopped coming. It was a situation noticed by the hospital's nurses, but few other people got to hear about it.

Indeed, she was still giving interviews saying that Peter was the most generous of men. Most meaningful of all was the statement: 'Our marriage, like a fine wine, gets better as it matures.'

He left hospital several weeks after first being taken there and forty-two pounds lighter. There was also a fifteen-inch scar staring him in the face every time he took off his shirt and looked in the mirror. But he kept the treatment and its cause to himself. For reasons that have never been satisfactorily explained, all records of his stay at the hospital vanished when he did. They did have a couple of souvenirs of his stay, however. Peter gave the hospital two colour television sets in gratitude for his treatment there.

The operation left him weak and still in considerable pain. But the biggest hurst of all was losing Sian and having to keep it mostly to himself. She had moved out of the Heath Street house and bought a home in Islington. Kate and Pat were staying on with Peter and so was their maternal grandmother. Both health and his marriage had taken a nose dive at precisely the same moment. This was not the case with his career, however.

The then Sir Lew Grade, having had to reconcile himself to not having Peter playing Judas, had other plans. Not knowing about the O'Tooles' marriage difficulties, he announced he was going to star Peter and Sian together in a series based on the World War I 'Red Baron' von Richthofen and his wife Frieda. Sian would have the bigger role, he said. But like so many other things, it didn't happen. It was a good enough reason to say that the idea had been dropped because Peter was clearly not well enough to go through with it.

He no longer drank at all, although he was developing an ever-growing thirst for strong tea. Sometimes, it was coffee. He still went into pubs—because the atmosphere had always been as much a heady drug as the booze. But now he never had anything stronger than a lemonade or a tonic water.

He was still in love with Sian and missed her dreadfully. But he never doubted that he had been principally to blame and that Sian was too brilliant, too attractive, to resign herself to being alone while her husband worked away from home, and went with other women.

She had also met a twenty-four-year-old actor—eighteen years her own junior—named Robin Sachs. His father is Leonard Sachs, who in recent years achieved considerable fame as the host of the British television series *The Good Old Days* in which he played the immaculately-dressed chairman of an old-time music hall. Robin and Sian had worked together in the play, *The Gay Lord Quex,* and now she and Sachs were in love.

The reality of Sian leaving Peter and finding a new lover were like body blows to O'Toole at a time when he was desperately trying to recover his health—and to keep the fact secret.

His state of health didn't alter his personality one little bit. When there was a good row to be had, he enjoyed it as much as ever. In October 1977, the old sailor O'Toole had a perfect solution to the problem of being left high and dry when the Hollyhead–Dun Laoghaire ferry—the principal sea link between Britain and Ireland—tried to sail without him. Peter arrived ten minutes before sailing time only to find the gangplank already drawn up. That was not something he was prepared to accept sitting behind a steering wheel. He told the ship's officers what he thought of them—and then when they still refused to bring down the gangplank, he snatched the ship's papers as they were being taken to the captain just before the 'off'.

'Who the fuck does he think he is?' Peter called when the officer protested. 'Throw me a rope or a ladder or something—for Jesus' sake.' No one supplied a rope or a ladder or 'something' and he held on to the papers.

He returned them only when the police arrived on the scene and then, he said, 'as a gesture of goodwill'. With such goodwill wars have been known to start. Peter left in a huff and, with a deep-sea diver who also had to be in Ireland quickly, chartered a plane to take him to Dublin. There, the argument continued—he took a taxi to meet the boat.

Peter invited the captain to discuss the matter with him—an invitation that was studiously declined. 'It's all part of the Irish–English contempt for people in the public eye,' grumbled O'Toole. As always, he tried to find more reason for encouragement in his work.

He went on location to make *Rogue Male,* a two-hour film for the BBC, based on Geoffrey Household's 1939 novel about an attempt on the life of Adolf Hitler.

175

The book had been a favourite of his since he first read it as a small boy, so making it was in many ways a labour of love—which was precisely what he needed at the time Sian was falling out of love with him. He played the Old Etonian intent on killing the Fuehrer—travelling across some of most beautifully rugged countryside both in Germany and rural England seen in a film since *The 39 Steps*. He played the part so brilliantly, and the film was such a coup—his first expedition into television since the very early days of his career—that he was being fêted by the BBC as their top star of the year. This involved the full panoply of publicity— including exposure on the Michael Parkinson Show— Britain's most popular chat programme. The only trouble was that he didn't know about it until he was sitting in a Dublin pub, watching a TV screen.

All the arrangements had been made, the slot finalised and the people involved told. Everyone, that is, except Peter. Rogue Male was not the unkindest thing said about Peter when the show's staff realised he was turning down what some people regarded as roughly equivalent to an audience with the Pope. 'Everyone seemed to know about it except me,' said O'Toole.

The reason he was in the Irish capital—not that Peter needed reasons to be in Dublin—was that he had gone back to the commercial theatre for the first time since *Ride A Cock Horse*. He had been sold on the idea of the lead in a new play by Peter King called *Dead Eyed Dicks,* a sort of who-am-I, rather than whodunit murder mystery. He was the guest playing detective in the moorland country house which becomes the scene for a whole series of stabbings, shootings and poisonings. But like a child at a birthday party, he has to dress up to play the game. First in trench-coat and fedora as Philip Marlowe; then in wing collar and dinner jacket as Lord Peter Wimsey and finally and ele-mentarily in deerstalker and cape as Sherlock Holmes. The crimes are solved as the three private 'dicks' would have done the jobs themselves.

Peter's idea was that the two-week season at the familiar Gaiety Theatre would be followed by a London run. He had invested in the play himself and since he believed the only subsidy that counted was 'asses on seats', he was going to make a success of it. But like many other things in the world of O'Toole, it didn't happen. It was another example of how much worse off he usually was when he worked on his own projects than when he got involved in other people's ideas. He had a better offer, he decided, to take the play to Australia. There, *Dead Eyed Dicks* was a dreadful flop and it died. Nothing more was said about it going to the West End.

He called Brenner to suggest that they work together again. He had an idea to put on some plays in Canada and the United States. 'He also told me that things were not right with Sian. He never thought anything like that would happen, because he still loved her tremendously. But he didn't blame her. He understood, although it upset him more than anything.'

And if that was not hard enough, he was virtually broke. Losses on *The Ruling Class* had been catastrophic. Most of his assets were tied up in trust funds for the children. He needed to make some money quickly. But before he set about achieving that goal, he wanted Nat to think about helping him with the theatre season over the Atlantic.

Brenner promised to think about it.

In the summer of 1977, Malinche Verdugo came to England. Two months later, she signed on for a stage-management course at the Bristol Old Vic school with Nat Brenner giving her his fullest attention, at Peter's request. 'She is a very intelligent girl,' Nat told me. 'Peter told her to study Shakespeare and the other greats. He wanted her to know *Lear* and *Volpone*.'

But Peter maintained that no matter what anyone thought, he still loved Sian. He told friends—although he never admitted it in public—that he understood why she left him. 'It's been a good canter.' Nevertheless, he said he was initiating divorce proceedings and was going to cite Mr Sachs as corespondent.

'Sian has given me the elbow,' he admitted at last. 'The Greasy E. It happens to a lot of men at my age. I harbour no rancour, only regrets. Divorce is a commonplace. It becomes a statistic. How many marriages go the full trip?'

His parents' had. They had been married forty-seven years. And then, just as things started crowding round Peter, the 'Captain' was involved in a road accident. If a good, honest, hard-working, hard-drinking Irishman could choose the cause of his death, then 'Patty' O'Toole would have asked no more than what happened to him at the age of eighty-six. He was knocked down by a car as he left a betting shop—and, instead of being left where he was, the car seemed to pick him up and throw him into the building next door. A pub. With the benefit of a shot of whisky, Patty seemed to be none the worse for wear, but he died soon afterwards.

So there was tragedy and trauma when Peter and Nat Brenner got round to discussing details of what was going to happen next. Peter had just made an inconsequential film that started life called *Coup d'Etat* and was eventually released as *Powerplay*. It was made in Canada. While in that country, he fell in love with the Royal Alexandra Theatre in Toronto, the sort of playhouse in which he liked to work more than any other. What he wanted Nat to do was to help him with a season there of *Uncle Vanya* and follow it with Noël Coward's *Present Laughter*—a play he had once done on television, with Coward himself advising (he did 'Don't Put Your Daughter On The Stage, Mrs Worthington' in the form of a soft-shoe shuffle). Peter thought that if it all worked, he would take up a number of offers to transfer the plays to Broadway.

Peter had always resisted offers from American managements. He didn't particularly like the States as a working base, and he continued to fear that the 'cornflakes boys' would manipulate him out of a fortune. He hadn't set up Keep Films to be dominated by Broadway accountants now.

But the offer they presented to him was tempting. He wanted Nat Brenner to set up the Toronto side of the deal for him. Brenner would direct *Uncle Vanya*—it was an insurance policy that left him content that it would be the kind of production he would want to do. But he couldn't do the season yet. He simply couldn't afford it.

He needed the 'economic smash and grabbery' that a big movie could give him and there was one on offer—to be made in South Africa. This was *Zulu Dawn,* a sequel to the Stanley Baker picture *Zulu.* Like most sequels it wasn't nearly as good as the original and had been produced in the fond belief that all the people who had enjoyed the previous film would go to see the new one without asking too many questions.

If Brenner agreed to help on the Canadian venture, he could afford to go off to South Africa with an easy mind. Brenner did agree and Peter left for Pretoria. He took Malinche with him.

Peter, with a small grey beard poking over the patrol collar of his scarlet uniform, fell off his horse twice and had to face up to African warriors using real spears—they laughed at producer Nat Kohn's suggestions that they use rubber ones. He was his usual, affable self to the other actors in the cast like Nigel Davenport and Simon Ward. But it was not a happy time. The film was poor and Peter knew that once again the critics would complain that he was wasting his talents.

But he was in love with Malinche and she helped him forget what had happened with Sian. And then there was a phone call. Malinche had been seriously injured in a car crash near Pietermaritzburg. She was admitted to hospital under the name Malinche Verdugo O'Toole. Peter was asked to explain: 'Miss O'Toole and I are kissing cousins,' he said, 'in the old-fashioned sense of the word. And when she comes out of hospital, we'll be doing a lot more of that.'

It was another blow to add to all the others and he was broken up by it. He stayed by her bedside whenever he

179

wasn't working. When she recovered, he said he was happy again. But he didn't look it.

When Peter arrived in Canada he was met by a shocked Nat Brenner. 'Peter looked terrible. He was thoroughly exhausted from his work on *Zulu Dawn* and his anxiety over *Malinche* and he looked dreadfully thin. He was terribly on edge.'

It was not an auspicious start to the tour. In Peter's absence, Brenner had organised dates for the plays at the internationally-prestigious Washington Centre, followed by Fort Lauderdale, Florida and Chicago. Broadway managements were straining at the leash to book him, too. There were also several invitations from Hollywood studios for Peter to consider working for them in the movie capital, but his distrust of the big studios, which had prevented him going there before, remained.

Toronto was a different matter because the Royal Alexandra was a wonderful theatre 'and I love old playhouses. I have no desire to mesmerise concrete in London'.

Uncle Vanya opened and did splendid business. But then Peter and Brenner had a row. O'Toole didn't like his production. There were too many mistakes. The one-time student had decided that the time had come when he knew more than his old master. In an atmosphere that was heavily-charged, Brenner—whose wife was now seriously ill—flew back to England.

Peter felt that he would now like to play Astrov instead of Vanya. And so that role was now his for the remainder of the tour. Peter was on his own. He did *Present Laughter*—and again, it was a huge success, with Roderick Cook directing. He took it to Chicago, where he was hailed as the brilliant actor who had thrilled movie audiences for years.No one could understand why he had never played on a live American stage before. They kept on wondering.

Present Laughter had a mixed Chicago reception. The London *Daily Telegraph* sent its critic Eric Shorter along to see such an important event as Peter's American debut—and after seeing the performance at the vast Studebaker Theatre asked: 'Whatever happened to Peter O'Toole?'

O'Toole, he said, 'managed to give a divertingly ambiguous impression of a matinée idol walking through a role which is almost actor-proof, suggesting sometimes that he was counting the house and at others that he was just a little bored. He did not play so much with his tongue in-cheek as with it almost out.'

During the Washington run, Peter decided he had had enough. He wasn't going to fulfill the rest of the tour. There was another film to make—and this time it was again in Rome.

Bob Guccione, head of the *Penthouse* magazine and club empire, had decided to film a story of ancient Rome, called *Caligula,* which was as near to hard pornography that the commercial cinema had ever seen. Its scenes were so racy that it took two years—and another row with the management—to get a London release. Peter was to claim afterwards that the picture was reworked after he had completed his scenes as the seventy-six-year-old, syphilis-ridden Emperor Tiberias.

The presence of Sir John Gielgud added a certain *cachet* to doing the movie, but there isn't the slightest doubt that, money apart, it was the last film anyone valuing his prestige and career should have allowed himself to do. As far Mr Guccione, he claimed that Peter was 'never sober enough to know what he was doing' all the time the film was being shot. Peter immediately cried 'lies' and said he was still firmly nailed to that wagon he had ridden since his operations.

Peter also upset Mr Guccione by announcing he was going into the magazine business himself. It was only a joke, but the man who had taken on *Playboy* at its own game wasn't amused by the thought of competition from a publication O'Toole swore he was going to call *Basement* which would include a 'Rodent of the Month' and 'Toe Rag of the Year'.

He didn't apologise for 'earning a shilling in a blue movie', as he put it afterwards. 'I'm a professional. If I've got a job to

181

do, I do it.' It was 'sordid, boring rubbish, entirely unerotic'. But it earned him his shilling—or two.

He said he didn't know it was going to be a blue movie until Mr Guccione changed the original Gore Vidal script, three days after they were all assembled. The director and the script were abandoned and Peter was asked if he would mind 'improvising Tiberias'. Since he was only going to be there now for six days and it no longer seemed worth worrying about he said yes and he and Gielgud simply began enjoying all the naked bodies around them—and ended up comparing operation scars and counting the money they would make.

But Peter's relationship with Guccione didn't help make the film any better. He knew what was going on. Some of the other actors didn't realise they were in a blue movie at all—until they discovered that heads being photographed in the foregrounds of one orgy after the other were supposed to belong to them.

Peter didn't get on any better with the director Tinto Brass, whom he persisted in calling after the British industrial giant, Rio Tinto Zinc. He complained that the only English that Brass could speak was 'turn over', when he wanted the cameras to start and 'are you finished'? Peter also insisted that on the first day of work, Brass asked him: 'What you want? How you like to be paralysed in picture?' O'Toole says he replied: 'Anything you like, Smiler.'

To make things even more bizarre, Peter was given a bodyguard on the film presumably to protect him from the paparazzi if not to protect the paparazzi from him. There were about a dozen men, all naked apart from silver-coloured Robin Hood hats, following him wherever he went. There was also a naked girl who attached herself to Peter without too much complaint from him. He called her 'Betsy, the Collapsable Crutch'.

Had he been clever he would have forgone the shilling.

But *Caligula* seemed yet another example of the way things were going for him. He decided to spend a lot of time alone, back in Ireland or in Hampstead, even though Malinche did seem to be right for him. What was more, he said he enjoyed it. 'I don't mean that if there was a bit of fun going on up the street, I wouldn't have my knickers on and be out of here like a shot. But mostly, I'm content to stay here.'

In a way he was having to face up to a double 'marriage' break up. In May 1978, his association with Jules Buck came to an end. 'It was one of those things. We had a very happy relationship,' said Buck. In truth, the relationship had become very strained. It wasn't easy for a businessman like Buck to deal with an artistic temperament like O'Toole's, particularly at moments of domestic upheaval. In August 1979, the divorce from Sian came through. There was nothing about it as old-fashioned as Peter citing another man. The divorce was granted to Sian—on the grounds that she and Peter had not lived together for two years.

There were girls who have claimed to have had affairs with Peter, including one young coloured woman whose name had been linked with ex-King Constantine of Greece. She said that O'Toole and she had made love in the middle of the night, only to have it all broken up by Peter insisting on dancing the tango. He then gave her a ticket to Ireland with instructions that she stay at the Connemara house.

The alleged romance was short. Peter wasn't really interested. For the moment, he had Malinche. 'I just want to sit around and make love to my lady,' he said. 'I don't really think of the unhappiness or the domestic life I once had. I am not an optimist so I just think that things could be worse.' Besides which, he had learned to boil a kettle, if not an egg.

Newspapermen were describing him as the 'Faded Golden Boy' of the British theatre. There were times when he felt it. The divorce finalised, Sian married Robin Sachs on Christmas Eve, 1979. Peter's mother-in-law, Mrs Sally Phillips, continued to live at the Hampstead house, helping to look after Pat who was at school in North London. Kate had by now begun to fulfil her father's chauvinistic dreams by starting university in Ireland, the world-famous Trinity College, Dublin.

Peter's own career, meanwhile, showed signs of pulling itself together. There were a number of projects being talked about, all of which seemed to offer more in terms of working satisfaction than a hundred *Caligulas* with or without collapsible crutches. There were two television series and a new film. If he had shown reluctance to work in TV before, the success of *Rogue Male*—to say nothing of the series in which Sian shone, to his continuing pride—now seemed to indicate that the smaller screen had a lot to commend it. One of the TV ideas had the stamp of the spectacular about it, which meant money. The other appealed in a different way. It was going to be Irish television's biggest ever attempt at a major special. The first offer was for a major part in *Masada,* the story of the heroic siege, with the Jews holding out on a mountain top near the Dead Sea. He would play a Roman. The second was *Strumpet City,* a story of poverty in Ireland. He would play a trade unionist. He said yes to both.

First, however, there was a film to make. It, too, was an American project. The only difference between this and the pictures he had made for Americans before was that this time he would actually have to film in the movie capital. *The Stunt Man* was about pictures—and the location was a Hollywood studio. There was just no way it could be made anywhere else. Besides, the money was good. The story was appealing and there was a whiff of nostalgia for his own early stunting days about it. He said yes, to that, too.

Peter moved into an apartment in the unfashionable part of Hollywood. It guaranteed a certain amount of privacy which he would not have been allowed in a Beverly Hills Hotel bungalow. Another reason was that it gave him an opportunity to 'feel' part in the sort of suburb where most of the lesser Hollywood people lived.

The last letter he had had from Sian told him to see a film called *Freebie and the Bean* directed by Richard Rush. He saw the film and agreed it was superb. Shortly after that, Peter was feeling bored at a party and decided to amuse himself by doing somersaults in the middle of the floor. When the fun of that exercise had exhausted itself, a man introduced himself to Peter saying he was a film director and had a script which he had written and would like to direct with Peter in the lead. It was called *The Stunt Man* and the director was Richard Rush. After seeing the *Freebie* film, it was a good enough introduction.

He played the director, a character variously described as being based on John Huston and Orson Welles, although Peter had to say he thought more of David Lean when making the picture than anyone else. Richard Rush had put about seven years' work into the film which he had written himself.

Even after the movie was finished and Peter was back in England, he became obsessed with stuntmen and the work they did for the sake of making a film that much more realistic. When he heard that a German stuntman had been killed making a leap from the Golden Gate Bridge in San Francisco, he booked himself into an hotel in Bristol—not to go back to old climes, but so that he could study the famous Clifton suspension bridge from the hotel window and work out how the stunt could have been done more safely.

O'Toole saw the director Eli Cross—he began to call himself Old Rugged Cross—as a crazy, appallingly dressed, very funny, and very human person. It was perhaps the best thing Peter had done since *The Lion in Winter*—and it stayed on the shelf for two years and would have remained there had there not been a certain happening that made the name Peter O'Toole news all over the world.

Before that, there were the TV series. *Strumpet City* was hardly a great success. Peter went to the Monte Carlo Television Festival himself trying to sell it—as much a gesture on behalf of Ireland as an attempt to win buyers for himself.

He wasn't very successful. The series was eventually bought for the United States and British television viewers saw it, too. But the word was that the purchase was made because Brtiain and Ireland were Common Market partners and the Irish had complained that not enough of their

185

material was getting exposure across the sea. It was a seven-part series in which Peter was brilliant as the dignified, composed and low-profiled James Larkin, an old Labour leader who had been a friend of his father, the 'Captain'. But strikes set in the dismal Dublin of the early years of the century weren't calculated to have a great deal of mass appeal.

Nevertheless, Peter's appearance at the Monte Carlo Festival was a wild success. If his star had been fading for some time, it now gave every indication of shining brightly again. He was dined by Arab television moguls who said nice things about *Lawrence* and allowed themselves to say some admiring words about the Irish, too. Princess Grace invited him to dinner at her palace. He was being hailed as the number-one attraction of the festival, even if *Strumpet City* wasn't.

But the series was something of a breakthrough. As he said, not so long before this very first Dublin-made TV series was conceived, an actor named Peter O'Toole playing an Irishman on the screen would have been expected to have red hair and carry a shillelagh. All Peter carried around with him was a lean and haggard look that was just right for everything except making money.

Nor were his other troubles all behind him—although he was now proudly saying that drink was a crutch he was glad he'd thrown away. But most men need a crutch of some kind and he no longer had one. As he told one journalist: 'I tried marriage. I had quite a lot of practice and performance. I am not in any hurry to remarry.' He didn't have anyone in mind to marry now, either.

After going on holiday with Malinche to Los Angeles, their love affair was now over, but he kept it to himself. There were other women in his life, but now that he was single again, no one seemed to take a great deal of notice. It was 1979 after all. His health wasn't as robust as his close friends would have liked it to be. He still looked The Bone that Sian had described in happier times. And there were more difficulties with his eyes. Halfway through the shooting of the

Masada series, he was flown to London for another operation to remove a cyst.

Masada itself, however, looked good. Having sharpened his Roman teeth—if not his Roman nose—in *Caligula,* he seemed a good choice for *Masada,* one of the biggest spectacles made for American television yet. He was to play a particularly nasty Roman general, Cornelius Flavius Silva, a man known to have gone on to Rome—via Alexandria—in triumph, although until he died there was no other mention of him in history.

It was again the time of Tiberias, although this general was much more in control of himself than the ageing emperor Peter had played before. He looked good in a toga, was sufficiently commanding to make the role and the series his own once he first appeared on the screen.

It was back to the desert for him again—only a stone's throw but a political world away from the site of his activities in the Lawrence film. This one was shot on location at Masada—and in Israel. He didn't wear the Star of David his mother had given him but it would have made him welcome had he done so. Not that any talisman was necessary. It was all a great success.

'I have a feeling,' he said after the series was completed' 'that in *Masada,* General Silva will wipe T. E. Lawrence away.

It didn't. But there was something on the horizon that soon would. No more would he be instantly identified with the white robes and desert sand that had haunted him for nearly twenty years. Now there was something else in view which *would* wipe the 'curse' of *Lawrence* away. Instead of his name being coupled with the colonel's every time someone somewhere wrote something about him, there would be a new title which would automatically spring to mind. But within weeks, he would wish with all his heart—and those of not a few thousand fans and admirers—that *Lawrence* was the only thing he had to live down. It had, after all, been a triumph.

Now, though, he was to be saddled with a reputation born the night he opened in what superstitious actors have always said was the unluckiest play ever written. It was supposed to be so unlucky that Peter himself wouldn't even pronounce its title. He was going to star, he said, in *Harry Lauder*. But it wasn't going to be the life-story of a great Scottish comedian—although there were people who laughed a great deal when they saw him on the stage. Too many, in fact, laughed, because *Macbeth* wasn't supposed to be funny.

Fourteen

IT ALL SEEMED such a wonderful idea. Peter was going back to the Old Vic, the theatre where he always thought he belonged, the place where he had had that first audition, the spot where no one would again charge he was wasting his time with inferior material. For whatever else anyone could say about *Macbeth,* they couldn't possibly say it was inferior. People just didn't sneer at Shakespeare.

For O'Toole himself it looked like the crock at the end of the rainbow. Not of gold, he wasn't searching for that. But of self-respect, of regaining the image that was his as Crown Prince and—who knows?—perhaps being invited to take the throne, too.

The Old Vic had suggested not merely that he play the lead in *Macbeth,* but that he become associate director of the company, too. He would have an office in the theatre and, after all this time, be welcomed back with a warmth that was reserved for a very few. It happened at the lowest point of his career. The details were finalised between the play in Toronto and the trip to Israel to make *Masada.*

If Peter had wanted it a little less keenly; if he had studied the ramifications a little more closely, he and the people who cared about him would have been a great deal happier. As it was, Shakespeare's play of murder and intrigue became a tragedy of proportions the Bard could never have anticipated; a disaster that was shouted from the front pages of newspapers on five continents. For the first time in memory, a play by Shakespeare was the main item on television news broadcasts and on the covers of magazines on both sides of the Atlantic.

Peter knew it wasn't going to be easy. And it wasn't just superstition—although he ran round the room looking for wood to touch whenever anyone had the gall to mention the name that Shakespeare gave the play in the first place. And he allowed himself, long before it opened, to say that there was something 'evil' about it.

'What's left of my insides are churning over at taking on *Harry Lauder,*' he said. And every time he talked about doing it the way he thought Shakespeare would have wanted it done, his brow became bathed in sweat.

'Sometimes, when I'm just scanning the text, words I've known by heart for decades, I sense new meanings.'

He often felt he had reason enough for those thoughts about evil and all the talk about the 'curse' of *Macbeth*. The day he drove to discuss the play with Frances Tomelty, the Irish actress he wanted for Lady Macbeth, he crashed the car into a stone wall. 'The Toyota almost fell into the Atlantic,' he said afterwards. It happened on a Friday the 13th.

He described it to Michael Owen in the London *Evening Standard* as almost a matter of life or death to him. 'I'm starting a new life. There is no point doing anything in the theatre unless you really feel committed. The theatre is no place to experiment. There will be no tricks in this show . . . You don't need to bugger about with it.' (A message he could have learnt himself a little later on.) 'I know there is a risk. I know there will be expectations. That's fine with me. There has to be danger in theatre or it doesn't work. You can't play safe.'

It is doubtful if he had any idea of just how dangerous it was going to be, although he had told another writer: 'Every day of my life I've made mistakes.' But he was sure that he was going to help save the Theatre. 'The West End theatre at the moment is a shambles. I've got no time for the old men who run most of the commercial theatres. Grants have killed the initiative in the subsidised areas. If the theatre is to survive, it must survive in the market place.'

He had set about doing his homework with *Macbeth* just as he had with *Uncle Vanya* and everything else. He worked alone in his study in Connemara, looking out to sea and reading all he could about the play, the part, the period. 'It is the only way to approach acting: unobserved, uninitiated, protracted, private study.' When he thought he had done enough, he invited other members of the cast to Ireland to talk it through with him.

It is a matter for conjecture whether or not his fear was there when he had the first approach from Toby Robertson, the artistic director of Prospect Productions—a company long subsidised to tour by the Arts Council and now licensed by the governors of the Old Vic to occupy and run the Old Vic itself and call itself the Old Vic Company.

What is certain is that the invitation to come to Waterloo Road was grabbed with open arms.

Robertson had read a newspaper report which said that Peter wanted desperately to come back to the Vic. The idea appealed to the theatre at a time when it could have done with a boost. It was in dire financial straits and there was constant talk of having to shut down. O'Toole, he reasoned, would not only bring his art and talents to the theatre, but he was probably still a strong enough name to have crowds lining up at the box office.

In 1978, Robertson told Peter that he was now in charge of the Old Vic. 'How would you like to come and do some work for us?' he asked. Correspondence was exchanged and telephone calls were made. Peter told the artistic director that he had a great ambition to play in *Macbeth*. But he also believed that it should be part of a repertoire for the company. Among the other things he had planned for it was his old staple, *Uncle Vanya*—only this time, he would direct himself. Plainly, what he had learned from Nat Brenner was enough to convince him that he could do it better himself than anyone else.

There was the old problem of time. He didn't want to commit himself to long periods of work for the Old Vic alone, but taking it into a new repertoire season would be enough. He could see *Macbeth* on its way and then, when it was soundly on its feet, he could have the days free to direct *Uncle Vanya*. It seemed a marvellously sound idea—and Robertson jumped at saying yes. Of course, things didn't work out that way. And until now, the reasons for all the troubles—despite the rash of publicity in which they were greeted—have been shrouded in mystery.

The first indication that there might be trouble ahead came when a company 'spy' returned from Canada with a report that she didn't like O'Toole's *Uncle Vanya*. Jane McCullough, the writer wife of Toby Robertson, had been sent to Toronto at company expense to give a first-hand report of how he had handled the play at the Royal Alexandra Theatre. It wasn't a move calculated to make for good relations between the theatre and its star. Certainly, it didn't do a great deal for the Old Vic's confidence in what O'Toole was going to do with *Macbeth*. She saw two performances there and came back—according to Andrew Leigh, now administrator of the Old Vic Company and formerly administrative director of the theatre—saying that she was concerned about Peter's stamina; and wondered whether he had the strength to manage the two plays in repertoire.

Then in July 1979, something else happened on the stage of the Old Vic itself. It is a theatrical tradition that a much-thumbed red cloth-covered copy of *Hamlet,* originally owned by Forbes Robertson at the turn of the century, should be handed to the man generally considered to be the most significant Prince of Denmark of his day—and, what is more, presented by its previous custodian.

Now it was Peter's turn to hand over the book to Derek Jacobi who had just been acclaimed as the great new Hamlet.

It was a gala evening, with not a seat (priced at twenty pounds) left empty in the house. But it was not a brilliant success for O'Toole. He rambled, he searched for words—

192

even apologised for making *Lawrence of Arabia* which only the people in the know from the National Theatre appreciated—and he made what some of the authorities in the Old Vic considered to be a mistake that virtually was in contradiction of Holy Lore. He paid tribute to 'Miss Horniman' when he meant Lilian Baylis, the much-respected and revered founder of the Old Vic (who, incidentally, died during a production of *Macbeth* at the theatre). Miss Horniman was founder of the British repertory movement.

It was the sort of mistake that almost anyone could make on an important occasion when nerves are likely to be frayed. But Toby Robertson chose to use the speech as another cause for doubt. Could O'Toole, he asked other executives in the company now, manage the very much more demanding role of Macbeth? It was not a question that was likely to sweeten relations with the star.

The matter was raised with Peter's lawyers who said that he could do the work perfectly well. When O'Toole himself got to hear about it, he was furious. Nevertheless, Andrew Leigh was asked by Robertson to negotiate a contract which would give Peter the title of associate director for a year, guarantee his services in *Macbeth* and say that he would be given the option to direct another play in the season.

The title of associate director was intended to be a loose one. It gave him total production rights over *Macbeth* and meant he would be available as and when both he and the theatre chose, to play and direct over the next few, but unspecified, years. They were, says Leigh, 'opening proposals'. No attention was yet to be paid to the way the productions were to be implemented. Negotiations with the lawyers proceeded. Quite unexpectedly, at one, Peter himself was present. He was on his way to Israel to make *Masada.*

This was the meeting at which Andrew Leigh, as administrative director—since there were no Old Vic lawyers present, it was his job to deal with the less pleasant details—was instructed to tell the O'Toole solicitors that there were serious doubts about their client's stamina and health. With Peter himself present, it was not a happy session.

Peter was furious. 'It's a breach of trust,' he declared, reported Leigh, who told me how uncomfortable he felt. 'I didn't think it was dirty work (having to make the statement about his doubts) because I didn't know what had gone on before. But I was certainly made to feel it was dirty work by Peter's reaction. He also said it was a breach of contract, and a breach of just about everything known to man.'

'I wasn't sure if he really felt hurt about it at all. It couldn't have come as much surprise—the press had been saying for years that he was infirm—that a member of the profession now said so, too. I can't believe that he was hurt, but I think he was surprised. It was the first he had heard about it. I don't think anyone had mentioned it to him before.'

Peter stormed out of the meeting in a furious rage—'although I didn't hear him use any bad language. Whatever it was he did say, it was a fine actor's performance.'

The rows and the doubts went on for weeks—with Toby Robertson refusing to give way. He told Leigh that he was convinced that Peter could only manage *Macbeth* and nothing else in repertoire. Meanwhile, O'Toole was writing letters from Masada saying how he was thinking of doing nothing else but the Old Vic season and that he was in perfect health—letters that the lawyers were showing at regular intervals to Andrew Leigh and other people in Waterloo Road.

Eventually, however, says Leigh, 'we drew up a set of terms which met with everyone's agreement. Peter conceded that he didn't have to do *Uncle Vanya* in repertoire. Everything else was also agreed. He would have dressing room number one and there would be no trouble with money.'

That last detail indicated fully just what Peter's priorities were. He would be paid no more than one hundred pounds a week while in rehearsal, and two hundred during the performance. 'It must have cost him a fortune to work with us,' said Leigh.

The dressing room was specified without any particular requirements being listed. Just before he moved in, however, he asked for it to be painted red—blood red. 'By this time, we had got to know him. We agreed to it after some discussion.'

But it wasn't all going to be that easy. Above all, there were the problems of raising the money. Just a short while before *Macbeth* got under way, the theatre was forced to borrow £400,000—the projected deficit at 31 March 1980. So it had to be covered by the prospect of obtaining revenue through ticket sales—as well as by the Arts Council grant.

Meanwhile, the Arts Council indicated that they would not object to seeing Toby Robertson replaced. They did not insist on it, but said they would not be sorry to see him go. Robertson had been artistic director for sixteen years and now there were disagreements over finance.

It happened during the time that the Old Vic was touring China with their production of *Hamlet*. Robertson had flown over to Peking to see the play at just the moment the directors of the Prospect had called a meeting to discuss the desperate financial situation. It was in the Chinese capital that Robertson was told he was sacked.

Timothy West, himself an actor with a considerable reputation, was invited to take his place and signed a two-year contract, starting in January 1980. A few years earlier he had received great critical acclaim in the name part in the *Edward VII* television series, and there had been a number of other achievements.

The appointment left the way open for changes to be made should they be deemed necessary. The contract with O'Toole had not yet been signed, and even if it had, it would have been framed in such a way to specify that the star would act as associate director to Tony Robertson. Now that Robertson was no longer in office, a new ball game had begun. Did the arrangement with O'Toole remain in force?

Timothy West took the hot potato in his own hands. He said he was shortly going to Hollywood to play the part of Vespasian in . . . *Masada*. He was sure he would meet Peter then and they could discuss it. And meet in Hollywood they did.

There was an extremely useful and encouraging discussion—although West thought that O'Toole's feelings about the theatre were somewhat old-fashioned. But he was encouraged about a great deal. As he told me: 'We got on well enough. I was very impressed by his enthusiasm and his ideas about *Macbeth*. About other things, I wasn't quite so impressed. It seemed to me that he didn't have all the necessary knowledge about contemporary subsidised theatre practice.

'For instance, he was very, very mistrustful of the Arts Council, which ironically, of course, he was to be proved right about. But we had worked very closely with the Arts Council and it was very necessary for us to provide a programme which was suitable for touring, which was possible within a certain kind of budget and which was attractive both for an Old Vic and a UK regional audience—to say nothing of audiences abroad.

'Andrew Leigh and I had a plan to do this in an economical way—although Peter really didn't understand it.

'I have to say that when I was in Hollywood, I didn't interpret it like this. He seemed content to let me cope with the day-to-day production work and future policy. He said he was going to work very hard for *Macbeth*.'

Their relationship seemed to be all set for West to take on a role similar to that of a film producer, with Peter being the star and in most ways the director, too.

West had returned to London, believing they could quite reasonably go ahead with the whole thing. But he told me: 'I was given a situation in which I could either accept the contract as it now stood—although because of an impasse with Peter's lawyers it had not yet been signed—or reject it. There was no way I could alter any of the wording. It was

196

made very clear to me by the Prospect board that if I really wanted to back out of it, I could. It was also suggested to me that that could be inconvenient and lead them open to legal action.'

The whole idea didn't seem such a bad move at the time. For one thing, both men were delighted with their choice of director, Jack Gold, the same man who had worked with Peter so happily in *Man Friday*. Said West: 'I had enormous respect for Jack Gold and his ideas seemed very sensible. He had worked with Peter before and they got on well.'

The troubles seemed to start when Jack Gold said he wanted out. There was no question of any rows or disagreements. He had simply had a better offer which he felt he couldn't refuse. Timothy West couldn't refuse him either. 'I've never known an occasion when a director works well doing something he doesn't want to do,' he said. But when Gold went, an insurance policy vanished, too. There were other problems on the horizon—although not all were immediately recognised as such.

Peter had in tow a Mexican inventor who had, he claimed, produced a system of making scenery from something resembling a huge balloon—so compact, in fact, it could fit into a car boot and then be inflated on stage. No one knew of the difficulties that would bring until several weeks later.

For the moment, the first official meetings between the Old Vic management and Peter's representatives had seemed to go off swimmingly. This was particularly true of the meeting at which everything was finally signed if not officially sealed. Andrew Leigh says it was 'very pleasant'. Peter had come from a rugby international game and was in superb form, accompanied by his close friend Sir John Ackroyd.

Now it was a question of waiting for the play. It was already being publicised in the press—with Peter himself saying again that *Harry Lauder's* reputation worried him, but he was glad to be one of the actors who were helping to subsidise his favourite theatre, the only kind of subsidy he found acceptable.

'Just everything is special about this place,' he told Michael Owen in the London *Evening Standard* in August 1980, little more than a month before the play was due to open.

'We've done the homework, done the scholarship, we are in good shape. It's going to be brilliant.'

By that time, the Old Vic people knew that it wasn't and the word had already begun to filter through London. But when the deal was signed, few had any inkling of the trouble that awaited them. 'Certainly,' said Andrew Leigh, 'I never had any doubt that we were going to see something very exciting, something very remarkable. There were twinges of doubt, not so much about what he would do himself but what other people were going to do.' And they started doing it.

But the big problem for the moment was that of finding a new director—a matter that didn't seem to worry Peter very much at all. 'The only thing that directors are for,' Andrew Leigh says he told him, 'is to make sure that people don't get in my way.'

'That was when I got my first real twinge of doubt,' said Leigh.

There was another moment, too, when the two men were sitting in Leigh's office, discussing the whole concept of *Macbeth*. 'He began to talk about medieval magic, a fey sort of magic involving fairies and he said that was what he thought *Macbeth* was all about. He gave me an exposition of his views that I thought was totally illogical and difficult to accept—because I had always thought of *Macbeth* as being about the corruption of power.'

There were also the problems of financing the enterprise. As Timothy West told me: 'Like most people who have responsibility for one production only, and really just one production, he wanted to spend a very great deal of time, money and resources on that one production and didn't care very much about what else was happening.'

Money was to be a continuing problem. But the hardest of all, to start with, was finding a director. Peter refused to work with the man nominated by Timothy West. 'I can understand this,' said West. 'If you've thought very hard about one particular approach to a play for a long time, you're unwilling to jettison this when a new director comes along. On the other hand, a new director doesn't want to work with someone else's ideas.' Time began to run out.

The search went on in an atmosphere of near panic. All the 'star' names were tried, people like Jonathan Miller and Michael Blakemore, but none of them were, in the event, available. Peter even suggested Nat Brenner, but that wasn't acted upon. Nevertheless, he and Brenner did meet and talked about each other's conception of the play and the part. 'He looked in radiant health,' Brenner told me. 'He was no longer emaciated, but all puck and vim. I thought it looked as if everything were going to be marvellous. He was back fifteen years.' But it didn't last long. 'He came to see me a few weeks later. He had changed. His face was long and he was emaciated again. And it's in that face that you can see everything about him.'

Another director was mentioned and approached—and he said, yes, he would love to do it. But after his first meeting with Peter, he backed out. 'I can't possibly do it,' he told Andrew Leigh. 'His (O'Toole's) ideas about the play are crazy. I'd love to help . . .'

Timothy West maintains that there were other directors who reacted in the same way.

It was Peter himself who suggested Bryan Forbes. It was a wholly unconventional notion—for although Forbes has an enviable reputation in the cinema, his stage experience had been much more limited. But the suggestion was accepted warmly—and Forbes said yes, too.

An early priority to deal with was the question of sets. Enter again, at this point, the Mexican inventor who was going to be paid two thousand pounds in two instalments. His ideas of inflatable scenery seemed like a gift to a repertory company that was expecting to tour. Sets for a Shakespearean production that would go round the country and

199

then travel abroad would normally cost about twelve thousand pounds. So it seemed a good buy. The designer was also given a large rehearsal room in which to work.

'I must say that we felt vulnerable at the time,' said Leigh. 'Peter had felt let down by Toby's attitude to him and we thought we owed him something. The idea of paying two thousand from a debt of £400,000 didn't seem that desperate.'

The man worked for some time and then, finally, the company was invited to a demonstration. As Andrew Leigh describes it, what happened at that demonstration sounds very much like the scene from a television satire programme.

'We were shown a set that was supposed to represent battlements. But what we could see were black dustbin bags which had been taped together, lit by light bulbs in sockets which had been screwed into emptied, clean, tomato juice cans. There were red daubs on the plastic bags which made it look as though he had painted them with the tomato juice before emptying it out of the cans. They were kept waving in the wind like palm trees by a pump, operated by a petrol motor (on a licensed stage, remember). It was so noisy you couldn't hear anyone talk, let alone an actor on stage perform.'

A number of distinguished theatre people were there, watching the demonstration. Peter was as disgusted as any of them—and had the inventor and his invention out of the building in half an hour.

A short time after that, the Mexican—now the worst for drink—came back to the theatre and addressed a group of stage hands, telling them that he was a close friend of Peter's and that soon everyone would be kicked out and O'Toole and he would be in charge. 'You're just a crowd of wankers,' he said.

That word 'wanker' became an integral part of O'Toole's vocabulary during his stay at the Vic. Before very long, it was clear that he regarded everyone who wasn't 'on his side' as an enemy.

The play was to run in repertory, side by side with *The Merchant of Venice,* in which Timothy West was to play Shylock. Peter decided that everyone working on *The Merchant* was in the 'wankers' team'. The real trouble was that because the plays were being worked as part of the same repertoire, actors were expected to play in both productions. Expected by everyone but Peter, that is.

Before long, agents were ringing up the Old Vic office in general and Andrew Leigh in particular trying to sort out a maze of contradictions. Yes, they said, they knew they had arranged for their clients to appear in both plays, but those same clients were now saying that Peter O'Toole had agreed that they should not be in more than one production at a time. That opened up another festering wound. 'Peter was also a bit hazy about dates and was in the habit of offering the same part to two people at the same time,' recalled Timothy West. 'It was a problem that was anticipated,' West told me. 'The question of cross-casting was the subject of frequent memoranda to Peter, but they were almost invariably ignored. If I laid down the law, I was accused of unwarrantable lack of co-operation.'

However, it was true that Peter had the right to choose his own cast—although his contract stipulated that he should do it in consultation with Timothy West. 'He also told people it would be all right if they only came to the last week of rehearsal, or that they didn't have to do the four-week tour that we had planned. But principally that he didn't want them to work in two plays at the same time.

'People were told they had really major parts—only for me to be asked by Peter to release him from the obligation of employing them. He had changed his mind about them.'

But there were no real problems with Bryan Forbes. 'We found him co-operative, intelligent, charming, witty, amusing and helpful, and completely understanding of the financial matters,' said Leigh.

It was impossible, however, for that to be enough—as Timothy West told me: 'The real difficulty was that Peter's and Bryan's ideas about doing Shakespeare were not quite the same as ours. There was a very strong disposition to want precise geographical locations. "This is meant to be a bedroom, where's the bed? Where's the wardrobe?" People don't do it like that any more. It's a very quick play with twenty-six scenes. You can't bring the furniture on like that. You have to let the actors and the lighting suggest it.'

Eventually, a man was appointed—a designer whom Bryan Forbes had known and respected for his work in films, but who had never worked in the theatre before. 'A very nice man,' said Timothy West. 'But I could not see how his designs could work. We ended up with a compromise—which, like all compromises, failed totally. We ended up with a cheap—which wasn't cheap at all—looking set which sort of did for all the scenes.

'The amazing thing was Peter himself didn't have any really clear ideas, although I expected he would.'

There was a similar disturbance over costume design. A very eminent designer, Stephanie Howard, was brought in. 'And she was in despair by the end,' West said. 'His ideas were not very consistent. Good costume designers want consistency, with styles and colours, that sort of thing. But it didn't happen.'

Peter, West told me, said that his ideas for costumes had all come from *The Book of Kells*. 'Now this is where I had to confess terrible ignorance. "*The Book of Kells,*" I said. "Oh, yes," knowing it was going to be some dusty tome I would be able to look at in the British Museum. "Oh yes," I told him. "That's good, Peter. That's fine." '

He finally discovered what the *Book of Kells* was when Peter produced for him what West describes as 'a sort of children's book of Celtic mythology with a lot of rather crude line drawings of people with those helmets with horns sticking out on both sides and plates. It all looked rather like a fourth-form production of *Macbeth*. I told him that it wasn't good enough.

' "Oh no," Peter told me. "It won't be like that." He elaborated on his ideas which began to sound workable.' It wasn't long before he decided finally that they weren't workable at all.

Meanwhile, there were administrative problems, too. Peter refused the Old Vic's offer of an office in the theatre's annexe. 'It's like the Gas, Light and Coke Company,' he declared, referring to a venerable pre-nationalisation utility.

Instead, he installed himself in what had been Lilian Baylis's office—a room about the size of a largish cupboard—which used to accommodate his secretary-assistant, Sarah Bullen, as well. She was an actress, too, and by all accounts very fond of Peter. They were seen on a number of occasions to be sitting together and walking hand-in-hand. But their relationship was not to last. She was off to pursue her own acting career—she had already starred in a television series for Granada. While she was at the Old Vic, Peter paid her salary himself.

The difficulties just multiplied like rabbits. Peter gave press conferences without consulting the management. 'He said dangerous things,' recalled West, 'like the Old Vic was trying to lose its Art Council grant because it didn't want it. It was all very untrue. He wouldn't come to our own press conferences. In fact he built up a wall between *Macbeth* and the rest of the company—and wouldn't allow his "team" to come to them, either.'

The company had its own very efficient press officer and an assistant. Peter insisted on bringing in his own PRO, the American Ernie Anderson, a man of great experience both with Peter and with the media. But his appearance was not greeted with much delight by the Old Vic establishment.

The 'wankers in the annexe', as West himself jocularly now also began to call his team, were, it seemed, to be regarded as the public enemy.

There was a further problem in that West was excluded from all rehearsals. It was again the relationship between star and producer that had not been unusual in Peter's films.

But a strange thing was about to happen. The public were becoming aware that this *Macbeth* was going to be different—even if no one could yet say anything about its quality. A great many tickets had already been sold on the strength of Peter O'Toole's name and the management felt that he had them over a barrel of the blood he said he intended to spill in the production.

West himself thought that Peter was going to use much too much blood-coloured liquid in the play for his own good.

'No blood,' said O'Toole, 'no play.'

Peter had to get his way in this as in most things.

'I don't think,' said Andrew Leigh, 'I would ever allow an actor to have that much power over a production again. In retrospect, I know we were weak. But we were living entirely on borrowed money. We were in a financial vice.'

Peter liked to feel that he had made the company himself and that it was his own. The Old Vic people for their part found themselves trying to conceal from Peter matters that they had themselves initiated.

The first read-through of the play had been quite encouraging. In fact, everybody was very happy with the way the actors went through their paces. There were six more weeks to go before the opening night. It was an unusually long time, but this was well on the way to being a very unusual play.

The rehearsals steadily deteriorated and there were some unhappy people around the Old Vic building. A week in, the assistant director—provided by Timothy West to help Bryan Forbes—Cyril Kinsky, was fired by Peter for not working according to O'Toole's concept of the play. He passed notes to the actors, which is not what an assistant director is supposed to do. But he felt that the firing should have been done by Bryan Forbes. Before he left, he told West and Andrew Leigh just how badly he thought rehearsals were going.

The talk was now spreading ever faster through the London theatre community. Sir Peter Hall had by then decided he was not going to go to see *Macbeth* and a number of Peter's friends made the same choice, long before the first night.

Says Andrew Leigh now: 'The thing that depressed the actors most was that they couldn't see where the genius that was going to carry them through was going to come from. They were worried by the relationship between Timothy and Peter.' But there was a saving grace—the box office was tremendous. Strangely, there were no big rows between O'Toole and West. When they met, they were sweet reasonableness to each other. But Ernie Anderson says: 'Peter would not go near the building where West was. He desperately wanted to restore the Old Vic to its old glory.'

There was an atmosphere that seemed impenetrable when it came to the sharing of rehearsal time. More and more of it was consumed by *Macbeth;* less and less by *The Merchant.* Timothy West undoubtedly felt that his own 'baby' was being threatened. There was a distinct feeling about it all that Peter had refused to accept that Timothy West was the artistic director of the whole theatre. He was at best considered a partner; at worst, a rival.

'He never accepted that Timothy was his boss, although Timothy never behaved like one, it must be said,' recalls Andrew Leigh. It got to the point where they avoided each other. Sometimes, it seemed that they arranged their arrival and departure from their dressing rooms—which were opposite each other—so that they wouldn't collide. There were no occasions when voices were raised at each other, although there was correspondence between them.

In the last week or so, all efforts were placed on getting *Macbeth* ready. Before the opening, the costs were beginning to be added up. Sets and costumes were over budget to the tune of forty thousand pounds. Said Andrew Leigh: 'I take full responsibility for that. I signed for them.' But one difficulty, he remembers, was that Peter refused to let the costume department know his shoe size. None of the theatrical costumiers had a sample O'Toole shoe in their possession. He merely asked them to let him have pairs that he could try on. But that could only be done if they were specially made for him first. 'In the end, no fewer than fifteen pairs were made before we could get one pair that fitted him.' The fifteen pairs were later sold at auction.

The tension was telling on Peter. And there was another reason for anxiety. His mother, Connie, was seriously ill and it worried him desperately. She had a birthday in the midst of the rehearsals. Peter decided that, no matter what, he would take her out for a champagne lunch. Connie loved it. Peter stuck to mineral water.

She was not the only honoured guest to attend rehearsals which remained banned to Timothy West. At about the time that *Macbeth* had first begun to be talked about among theatre lovers in London, Princess Margaret expressed an interest in the play and attended an early rehearsal—doing the company's morale a great deal of good by saying how much she enjoyed it.

The Old Vic was closed for the last two weeks of August because O'Toole insisted on having the stage to himself for the fortnight immediately prior to the opening of *Macbeth,* a situation helped by a particularly disastrous week of a play by J. B. Priestley which was stopped in mid-run. Peter was still telling the theatre management that he knew his play would be a brilliant success, despite almost everyone else's reservations. Only he had all the answers. Leigh recalled: 'Peter kept telling us that he believed that everything the British theatre did was rubbish.'

The play was due to open on a Tuesday evening. There would be a technical rehearsal the previous Saturday and a dress rehearsal on the Sunday—much against most of the company's will because it would cost about two thousand pounds in overtime payments. Such are the workings of the modern theatre, there would be a preview before the first night.

It was when the dress rehearsal was held that Timothy West insisted on being brought in. This was one rehearsal he intended to see and—as he said—'they couldn't refuse me that. This was going to be an opening production by a new regime, so it had to be just right.'

'I went to it and was very distressed by what I saw artistically. There seemed to be no approach to the play at all. It didn't seem to say anything or take an attitude about the witchcraft or the world in which they lived, or ambition—all things which the play is about. There was no artistic line. I won't comment on Peter's performance because that wouldn't be proper—actors give the performance they want to give. But it didn't strike me that Peter, despite all his talk about his attitude to the play, was saying anything about it that was relevant or imaginative. It was just Peter saying the lines. There was a well-known ploy of actors saving their best for the opening night when they can astonish everyone. He might have been doing that. But what I saw I didn't think was right for a dress rehearsal.'

'I had a number of suggestions about the actual technical competence. There were too many soldiers who got terribly in the way and didn't know where they were going. Scenes were cluttered. Pauses were too long while nothing happened. And then there was the blood. There was much too much of it getting all over everyone.'

West made a list of notes. He took it to Bryan Forbes. 'He agreed with most of what I had to say. Except that he said he was in the difficult situation of not being able to do anything without Peter's approval. He thought that there was a very slim choice of getting that approval.'

West tried to see Peter himself. He refused. 'We then had to try to find a way of saving ourselves, or protecting ourselves from what I was now convinced was an appalling situation.'

West and Andrew Leigh met for an indigestion-provoking breakfast the next morning. West said he thought that they ought to cancel the play. He was talked out of doing so. But what was agreed by Leigh and others in the company was, in West's words, that 'we had to make it clear that this production was being made in a special way and by a special

207

agreement and that it should not be taken to imply that it reflected the standard, the attitude or the style that people could expect from the rest of the season'.

It was that move that was before long to cause the biggest row of all. West wrote a letter to the lawyers of both the company and O'Toole saying that he wanted to make a statement to that effect. It was agreed that a throwaway would be inserted in the programme, emphasising that *Macbeth* was 'under the control of Mr O'Toole'.

The preview was held as planned—an evening that not many who were there will easily forget. Joe O'Connor told me of his great distress at seeing the humiliation of his old friend. 'The choice he made was wrong,' he told me. 'He had been ill—and to play Macbeth you needed to be on top of your physical form. To do it, as he did, eight times a week, is astonishing. He should have played something like Angelo or Cassius—which he could have done brilliantly. But Macbeth is one part where you have no one to support you. Lady Macbeth withers very quickly and thereafter you're on your own. After all, Othello has Iago. Lear has Cordelia and Kent, and Hamlet has Horatio. Macbeth has no one. I can understand how lonely he must have felt. But there was also the challenge—and I can understand that, too. The mistake was simply trying to do too much. If only he could have been with someone, like Nat Brenner, someone he could work and laugh with.'

But the fact remained, nevertheless, that the O'Toole performance was almost unbelievably bad.

A theatre director told me: 'I was afraid that it looked as though he had gone mad. His conception of the play was incredibly misjudged. He seemed ruthlessly self-centred.' Peter declaimed in what was described as a loud monotone, while everything around him seemed to be awash in blood. When Shakespeare expected the audience to be hushed and shocked at the evil being wrought on stage, they were in fact convulsed in near hysterical laughter. The laughs began in the front row and ran to the back like a lighted fuse burning

its way to the barrel of gunpowder. The explosion came the
following night.

Fifteen

PETER HAS SAID that he always felt he was born to play Macbeth. Obsessed with it since he was fourteen, he wanted to lay the jinx that hung over him at that first failed audition, a memory that had never left him. But this wasn't going to be the time. As he went on stage he felt cold and tense, the kind of feeling he thought he had left behind him after that memorable, not to say sensational, other first night at Stratford exactly twenty years before. As he later described it, 'It was a curious mixture of mania and fear and zaniness. It is like a bell ringing for the start of a prize fight. Once you begin, you forget your own feelings.'

But he didn't forget those feelings on this occasion. And neither did the public. The word had spread again. *Macbeth* was worth a good laugh. The audience that first night in September 1980, who had booked primarily to see what they believed would be a performance of grandeur, stayed in many cases out of a kind of sadistic curiosity. Could it be as bad as they had been led to believe? They came to the conclusion that it was every bit as bad.

When Peter walked smack into a wall on his third exit on a largely darkened stage, whole sections of the audience appeared to be convulsed in uncontrollable laughter.

'Every night was agony,' said Andrew Leigh. At one performance Nat Brenner sat in the stalls—crying. 'It was a shambles. People would rather see Peter do something badly than watch someone else do it well,' he told me. 'He was a shadow of his former self. He was obviously so without energy. There was no conception to the thing.'

Part of the trouble was that it seemed so old-fashioned. For weeks, Peter had been walking around, like a child with a toy, carrying a model of the set which he thought would help rejuvenate the English theatre. Instead, it turned the Old Vic into the home of a whiskery melodrama. The set was filled with a series of platforms and steps—a technique that went out at about the time Olivier's *Hamlet* was being shown in the cinemas. It was an odd mixture of realism and stylisation with a realistic forest in the background fronted by steps which Peter and the other actors would suddenly climb, one foot on the third stair, one on the sixth, to make a speech.

(Ernie Anderson told me: 'Peter actually hated the set himself, but he went along with it out of loyalty to Bryan Forbes. He didn't think he had much choice at that stage.')

Even worse was the darkness. Blackouts hadn't been used to mark the changing of a scene in a Shakespearean play in two generations. But they were here—partly to allow the blood which had literally been stored in a bath to be mopped up.

The blackouts confused the audience—who on one celebrated occasion had to be persuaded by a stage manager not to leave. It wasn't an interval, he assured them. When it wasn't described as a melodrama, it was a Victorian pantomime.

The critics were merciless. Michael Billington said in *The Guardian* that he thought O'Toole spoke with a 'monotonous tenor bark as if addressing an audience of Eskimos'. And *The Times*'s Irving Wardle wrote: 'It gruesomely evoked the kind of thing one used to get from Sir Donald Wolfit on a bad night.'

With the exception of the *Daily Telegraph*—John Barber wrote of 'some rousing thrills and a knock'em down display of fireworks from a famous star'—nothing anyone said was less than unmitigatedly damning—although 'unmitigated' was the one word that the *Daily Mail's* respected critic Jack Tinker said he could not use to describe the offering. 'There is at least one thing to be said in mitigation,' he said and then proceeded to rub in everything Peter had heard for himself. He was the only actor 'ever to set me off in a fit of involuntary giggles throughout *Macbeth'*. He even said he thought that O'Toole's voice was a combination of Bette Davis in *Whatever Happened To Baby Jane?* and of Vincent Price 'hamming up a Hammer horror'.

'No wonder,' he added less than charitably, 'one has to suppress the urge to guffaw when such burlesque dignity is given its comeuppance . . . It is surely the most hilarious miscalculation to totter out of Duncan's death chamber covered from head to toe in bright red gore, clutching two dripping swords, and eventually gasp out the purely superfluous information: "I have done the deed." '

Never in his career before had Peter O'Toole received a notice of that kind. Previously the worst that had been said about him was that he had unwisely chosen material that was beneath his own talents. Now influential writers were spelling it out that the very actor they had previously acclaimed as brilliant and spellbinding was himself turning out a performance that was, to say the least, lacking.

Jack Tinker wrote about 'Bryan Forbes's British B movie approach to the entire production. His three witches are transformed into glamorous extras from some abandoned *Brides of Dracula.'*

The same critic commented the next day: 'If Peter O'Toole awoke yesterday with only his ego bruised by the reception of his lamentable Macbeth, he can count himself a lucky man. Time was when a performance of this spectacular ineptitude would have excited at the very least catcalls and an occasional cabbage from any discriminating audience.'

He also thought it might be a good idea to revive the idea of giving actors the bird—literally letting off a squawking bird from the gallery and watching it fly round the auditorium.

Peter might have been forgiven for thinking that that was precisely what Timothy West had given him. It was, West told me, 'the worst half hour of my life' as he stood in the theatre foyer watching the people go into the auditorium—'people like Irving Wardle (*The Times* critic) going in, giving me a thumbs-up sign when I knew they were going to see the worst play we'd ever put on'.

As he stood there, he was approached by a reporter from the London *Daily Mail* who had just read the note in the programme. 'He came over to me and said: "Does that really mean that you had no participation in the show?" I said "yes".' It was taken as a gesture of disowning the production, and set all the theatrical cats among the dramatic pigeons.

The paper reported his saying: 'Peter picked the production, the director, did the casting and it was entirely in his hands. I was not involved in this production.'

Having made his statement, West sat through the first act watching Peter O'Toole performing for some reason, he said, 'in plimsolles or rather baseball boots'. He still hadn't satisfied himself that the fifteenth pair would be good enough. 'I then left. I'd had enough.' Nor did he attend the first-night party. 'I went round and said nice things to the cast. Poor darlings, they were as worried as anyone. But I couldn't face them at the party.'

Within hours, his statement was in the first editions of the *Daily Mail* and being broadcast to the world by the BBC, who had picked it up from the paper.

The next night, Bryan Forbes—who had been quoted as saying 'It's a tough play, in many ways the toughest in the canon; the disappointments I shall read tomorrow'—made a speech from the stage attacking West's disloyalty; something that had never happened before. He described him as Judas.

'Ladies and gentlemen,' he said, 'as you already know, World War III was announced today' (a not too subtle way of showing his amazement that a theatrical first night had become first-page news). 'We are bloodied but not bowed.' And then as Peter stood, head down with the rest of the cast behind him, came the blistering attack. 'I've always thought that Judas was one of the least attractive characters in the whole of human history. I would therefore like to say that I don't disown my company or my stage crew or my lighting crew or my sound crew. On the contrary, I stand with them and I applaud them.'

Some members of the audience applauded with him. Others just stayed to laugh.

Peter himself managed his first smile for twenty-four hours. On the whole he was remarkably calm, reserving a few mild obscenities for the most blistering critics. Asked what he thought of being compared with Bette Davis and Vincent Price, he said simply, 'Not a lot.' But as for Mr Tinker he added: 'They are half-truths, truths, serious aberrations and lies. Reviews which are helpful, however crushing, are fine. But what can I do? It's fish and chip paper tomorrow.'

As for Timothy West—who by now had added: 'I don't know what can be done about Peter's own performance. To my mind, he wasn't giving a performance'—Peter said it was 'None of West's business.' He even at one stage called the artistic director, 'Miss Piggy', after the character in the Muppets television puppet series.

West also said: 'I think that possibly because Peter and Bryan are people who work mostly in another medium, they perhaps haven't kept pace with the way that classical theatre is moving.'

Of O'Toole, West told me he liked best the comment from a newspaperman who said, 'if West is Judas, it gives a fair idea of who Peter O'Toole thinks he is himself'.

Peter, still smarting, said: 'I've been insulted by experts before now. If he disowns this production, he'll be skint.'

Peter, however, did concede that the play wasn't perfect, 'but it will be better. I would never contemplate restaging it. I shall continue to have full artistic control. I am not going to make any changes. It'll be just as I want it in time. All the ingredients are there, but it hasn't come together yet.'

And, he added, one always had to expect trouble with *Macbeth*. He now pronounced the name. Even the Old Vic had always had problems with it—which included Olivier's performance no less than anyone else's. It was true that Sir

Laurence had had a very mixed reception and even lost his voice on the first night. Charles Laughton was booed.

He claimed to have warned the company to expect trouble. 'First nights are a modern form of bear baiting. A sophisticated form. Sometimes, I was pleased the way it was going. Other times, I wasn't. I knew the reviews would be bad. You only have to look at the record of the play and O'Toole. I didn't think they would be that savage.'

Peter was plainly disappointed. He had said of the play earlier: 'It is the greatest Shakespeare has written. It's blood and thunder.'

Certainly he did not think he was using too much blood. 'If we put on ourselves one-tenth of the blood involved in killing three humans, then we would be soaked. What we present on stage is a token offering.'

Two months later, ever frank when it was fairly safe to be so, he admitted that a lot of the problem had been due to his being away from the London stage for so long. 'I opened my mouth and a lot of rust poured out,' he said. However, Peter did think he had the last laugh: 'I would refer all cowards, all begrudgers and all the timid to look at the box office.' And it was true that as the notices got worse—and with the Sunday papers and other weeklies' reviews, the picture was mounting in unpleasantness—the lines outside the theatre were growing. The telephone wires to the box office all but burnt up with calls from prospective customers seeking no-longer available tickets. In two days, £200,000-worth of seats had been accounted for.

To be fair, Timothy West maintains: 'I don't think people came because they expected to see anything terrible. There were just as many who came to see our *Hamlet*. They came because Peter O'Toole was a very major star.' But he agrees that the reason they came is a subject for debate. The box office certainly benefited from the publicity.

Ticket touts who normally did their business selling impossible-to-get passes for anything from rock festivals to football cup finals, were for the first time in modern history offering tickets for the classical theatre—and Shakespeare at that. The only people who seemed to be bowing out from the competition were that normal staple of the theatre, school-children studying the plays for exams. Now, the teachers were having second thoughts and wondering whether Peter O'Toole's performance was really the kind of thing that would help with Certificate of Education examinations. But the youngsters who had already taken charge of the tickets themselves made use of them—with the same enthusiasm with which they might well have gone to just one of those rock concerts.

Peter's friends and associates continued to go to the Old Vic. Some went to see him after the performance; others thought it polite not to embarrass him by going. One man told me he thought it was 'appalling'. Frank Finlay sent a telegram apologising for not going. Nigel Stock said that he could not bring himself to see it. 'I wouldn't go along to glory in the disaster,' he told me.

From Connemara, Frank Kelly, who keeps a wine and spirit shop in Peter's Irish home town and with whom he had been spending quite a lot of time when there, came to see the play—an example of the loyalty and friendship which Peter always seems to promote. He didn't think *Macbeth* was very funny at all. 'I didn't laugh a lot,' he told me.

What none of them knew—and Peter has never said it publicly—was that there was one good reason at least for the horror show that *Harry Lauder* turned out to be. His mother was now dying. She nevertheless came to see the play—brought by ambulance. When she died during the run, Peter positively refused to allow the news to be published. He didn't want sympathy.

(Andrew Leigh commented to me: 'It just shows you how badly our relationship had sunk. No one knew about it. What a terrible state of affairs!')

His relationship with Sarah Bullen collapsed at much the same time—amid rumours that he was very close to the actress who played one of the witches in *Macbeth,* the attrac-

216

tive blonde Trudie Styler. Miss Styler has refused to speak about it.

All these events doubtless combined to cause his behaviour to be less than that of the relaxed star, confident in his stardom. The act of being on stage is always enough to excite him to the point of preventing his sleeping at night. And when he couldn't sleep even on pills, there were long middle-of-the-night walks through Hampstead Heath. When he didn't want to sleep, there were the constantly available transfusions of black coffee and strong tea. Solid food hardly seem to come into it at all. It was not a diet or a regimen calculated to make life easy for him.

Nor were the happenings of the third night, the Thursday when a woman, said to have spoken in a 'soft, Irish voice' rang the stage door to say that a bomb was planted somewhere in the theatre. The building was evacuated and members of the cast still in costume sat on the pavement outside waiting for instructions. They came less than half an hour later when everyone was invited back into the auditorium. But they didn't see the play. Instead, Peter—wearing part of his costume—came to the front of the stage and told them: 'The police are at the stage door.' (That was precisely what some people had been joking would happen after the reviews.) 'It is with the utmost reluctance that I beg everybody in this house to take it seriously.'

At that point Brian Blessed, dressed as Banquo, pointed to Peter and said: 'Ladies and gentlemen. Do come and see the show—because he is absolutely smashing.'

Peter himself was extremely distressed by it all. He said he felt he could have proved the critics wrong that very night. The next evening, he tried again—and got a rousing ovation from the audience, who, nevertheless, had done their own share of laughing.

At about this time, the board of directors of the Old Vic decided it was about time they put their own cards on the table—and took full responsibility for giving Peter the authority to take *Macbeth* along the road he chose.

217

Meanwhile, Toby Robertson had re-entered the scene. He made a slamming attack on Timothy West and said that his lack of co-operation had been more damaging to the play than all the bad reviews. None of this, however, was going to faze Peter.

To everyone's credit, the grumbles and the backbiting within the company seemed to fade at this point, although few people saw things getting any better. 'I must say I expected that Peter would get out of it,' said Andrew Leigh. 'I thought there would be the quickest medical certificate ever concocted on my desk on the second morning.' But it said a great deal for the O'Toole tenacity that this did not happen.

Not only was he going to stay with the play till the bitter end, but he was going to tour with it too. And not just in Britain. He was determined that there should be a tour of Europe; a celebration, as he put it to the management, of Ireland's recent entry into the Common Market, which would be personified by his own production of *Macbeth*.

By coincidence, at the same time, a well-known Dutch impressario, Dr Jan de Blieck, had said that he would like to organise a tour of the company in Europe in 1981. Peter said yes to the idea—and enthusiastically. However, he said that he only wanted to tour actual Common Market countries, and then it would have to be all nine of them.

The British Council were going to help with backing the project, and it all looked set up. Until, that is, the first night at which Jan de Blieck was present. 'Afterwards,' said Andrew Leigh, 'he was very non-committal. He said that he wanted some of the theatre managers who had already said they would take the play to see it first.'

But cancellations came in before that could happen. The first was the British Ambassador in Bonn who indicated that he did not think that O'Toole's *Macbeth* was a sufficiently prestigious representation of British culture for him to want it to be officially produced in West Germany. That was only after reading the newspapers. He did not come to see the play himself. Several weeks later, the British Council in Paris said the same thing, although they had originally planned to feature it as part of the celebrations marking the bi-centenery of the *Comédie Française.* It would be the only British contribution. However, the manager of the Tivoli Theatre in Copenhagen came to see it and said that he would continue to feature the play. It might have gone to Denmark, except that the British Council as a whole said they were no longer interested in offering their help. At that, Dr de Blieck pulled out and the whole Common Market tour fizzled out.

Ernie Anderson issued a statement on Peter's behalf in which he said that the notices for the show were 'so hysterical and brutal that it's not surprising that the people in Europe were influenced. They made news all over Europe. But I don't think Peter will have time to be disappointed'.

And there were still standing-room-only houses in the Waterloo Road and advance booking for a domestic British tour had gone so well that an unheard of thing happened. The Arts Council decided to book the Old Vic into huge two-thousand-seater theatres that normally filled up only with pre-London runs of American musicals—and then not always—or with visits from pop stars whose records were currently at the top of the charts. *Macbeth* would be playing at the Bristol Hippodrome—Peter's beloved Theatre Royal was much too small—the Liverpool Empire and similar establishments. Totally inappropriate, and it had never happened before to a Shakespearean production.

In fact, it was fair to say that not since Shakespeare was the most popular dramatist in the land, when he filled the old open-air Globe Theatre, had his work been such a sell out.

Perhaps the performances had improved, maybe Peter was more relaxed, or even that the people in the stalls and circle in the provinces were less sophisticated and critical. Whatever the reason, *Macbeth* was received much more enthusiastically than it had been in London. Much more significant, the critics seemed to like it, too.

Writing in the *Birmingham Post,* D. J. Hart said that Peter was 'magnificent', even if the production as a whole was 'static and ordinary'. The *Coventry Evening Telegraph's* Peter McGarry said that *Macbeth* in the hands of O'Toole was 'a figure of emotional substance . . . ever formidable'.

Peter himself said *The Boot—Harry Lauder* hadn't done him much good, so superstition demanded a new title; possibly it was *The Boot,* because it had kicked him so badly—was now all but polished into shape and was for ever more part of his own repertoire.

When the provincial tour was over, Peter and the company went back to their London 'home'. On 22 November—he remembers the date precisely—it was the best performance of all. 'Oh, the liberation . . . the sense of overcoming,' he said.

The play, all three and a quarter hours of it (no one really expected it would last for more than two and a half hours) went on and on, with Peter sticking with it all the way. He gave forty performances at the Old Vic itself without missing a single one.

At the end of the final performance, he kissed Frances Tomelty and said he was glad it was all over. 'But I'm very glad I did it.' Yes, he said, he had been very hurt by what the critics wrote. The performance and production itself were demanding enough without that. 'They really cut me.' But he didn't have very much respect for the critics anyway. 'I'll be around after they've gone.'

Harry Lauder had brought £400,000 into the Vic's funds, the precise amount which had been spent on the production, and which also represented the very sum that had been lent to the company by its bankers. But since there had been no profit, the debt remained outstanding.

It did not mean that all was now happiness and light in the relationship between Peter Seamus O'Toole and the Old Vic. On Christmas Eve, 1980, he resigned his position as associate director of the company—an office most people had forgotten that he held. He had worked terribly hard, he said, after the adverse notices, 'but for the people who currently run the Old Vic theatre, that is not enough and, therefore, I have today resigned my position as associate director. The public will be the final arbiters of what is Old Vic tradition and I hope that in future I will be able to serve it again.'

He said that he deliberately left the announcement until after the play was over—because that seemed the fairest thing to do. Analysing it all, his conclusion was fairly simple. It was, he said, 'without any question, the most difficult thing I've ever done. I knew when it was right. I knew when it began to come right.'

Timothy West said that the resignation was 'news to me', and that he had not been consulted. 'It was a partnership that never quite worked out.'

West saw the end of the road before Peter did. 'Peter came into my office before he left and said: "How about *King Lear* next year?" '

Despite everything, he wanted to have another go. West was not interested. 'I told him "no". Forcefully. And frequently.'

Peter left the Old Vic for the last time, saying that he knew it had been a success.

'In the history of the British theatre, there have been only three actors who have pulled it off—Macready, Garrick and Wolfit. And now me. It took time, but eventually it came together.'

Did the Old Vic itself feel sad? Timothy West says he does. 'I thought it was a terrible waste of a very good organisation. It should have been a very happy and progressive time—and many ways was—which was blighted by that particular episode. I think it will remain in people's minds for a long time and that is a pity.'

Andrew Leigh is more forthright: 'I don't think sad is the right word. I think he thought we were a bunch of wankers till the end.'

It was not a view totally shared by everyone else. Nor was it the end of the story. In December 1980, just as the play finished its run at the Old Vic, the Arts Council of Great Britain announced it was going to withdraw the £300,000 a year grant it had made for the theatre's touring productions. It was a blow from which it would not recover. The next year, the theatre closed.

'I am not sure that the fact that there had been all the trouble over *Macbeth* was the reason,' said Timothy West. 'I should like to think that it wasn't.'

Sixteen

AS HIS OLD RADA friends had noticed, you had to be brilliant to be that bad, and that may well have been the psychology behind what happened after *Macbeth*.

Other actors in Peter's position could have been expected to go home, licking wounds that hurt savagely, waiting impatiently for phone calls they knew would never come. In Peter O'Toole's case, the calls seemed never to stop. The people who thought he had snatched disaster from the jaws of triumph and opportunity sat back in amazement realising that he was a hotter 'property' at the beginning of 1981 than he had been at any time since *Lawrence of Arabia*.

There wasn't, of course, the same degree of satisfaction. People were interested in O'Toole for the same curiosity reasons that had kept the box office humming in Waterloo Road; not because they believed he was a great actor. And that was distressing, because Peter *was* still a great actor. But he was also news.

Proof of that came when he was rushed off to the United States to publicise *The Stunt Man,* more than two years after it was completed and, apparently, left to gather dust on the shelf. What it gathered now were rave reviews and it instantly became a kind of cult movie. In Britain, the reaction was more guarded. Arthur Thirkell wrote in the *Daily Mirror:* 'I welcome it as refreshingly zany entertainment.'

The image of *Macbeth* was, however, a long time fading. At the same time as the other papers were writing about *The Stunt Man,* the *Sunday Mirror* was recording his Old Vic

223

adventure as one of the 'Worst Shambles of 1980'—after President Jimmy Carter's failure to rescue the American hostages in Iran, his election campaign, the British Tory Party's monetary policy and the Moscow Olympics.

There was no evidence that the headline gave Peter too much worry. He was, however, concerned about the way his career had gone. In January 1981 he was telling the showbiz 'Bible', *Variety,* that he was very concerned he had not yet won his Oscar.

But there was a huge consolation. While the laughter of the Old Vic audience was still ringing in his ears, he heard he had just been voted Best Actor of the Year by the (American) National Society of Film Critics—for *The Stunt Man*. But the Oscar was the one he still wanted. 'I'd adore to win,' he said. 'Wouldn't you?' Once more, he got an Academy Award nomination, but even *The Stunt Man* was denied the actual Oscar. Still, it didn't seem bad, so long after a film had been completed, to have that sort of recognition.

Unfortunately, the night of the Oscar ceremonies left more questions unanswered—particularly about Peter's health. Was something wrong? He made a speech that night that sent ripples of embarrassment through the audience. For many it was inaudible and to those who did hear it, inarticulate. Was it just that Peter always found speechmaking difficult? A few months later, filming in New York, he was taken to hospital with an undisclosed complaint.

He still talked constantly about the future. He wanted to remake *The Bridge on the River Kwai* for a Japanese director who was going to see it from *his* country's point of view. It was a decision that did not endear him to Britain's Far East War veterans.

The entirely unexpected reaction to *The Stunt Man* made Hollywood a much more inviting proposition than it had ever seemed before—perhaps because the film community, in the fond belief that you are only as good as your last movie, were more interested in remembering his role as Eli Cross than they were that of Harry Lauder. Now in the autumn of 1981, a full year after the Old Vic, he was making another Hollywood film about Hollywood, *My Favourite Year*.

It was an opportunity for him to live out on the screen some of those fantasies he had had about being another Errol Flynn. He played a fading matinée idol—with a Flynn moustache—who was better with women and the bottle than he had ever been in front of a camera. It gave Peter an opportunity to use some of the fencing techniques he had picked up at RADA, for the star he played was fairly handy with a sword, too. The film contained flashbacks to some of the early O'Toole pictures, like *Great Catherine* and *Lord Jim* and for one movie-within-the-movie he had his face glued tight—to make him look twenty years younger. In some ways, he felt it. A cut-down version of *Masada* was even released as a large-screen epic called *The Antagonists*. But it hardly took a penny and in England, the press kept remembering *Macbeth*. Arthur Thirkell said this time in the *Daily Mirror*, 'I urge you to see it for O'Toole's performance. He's the lad to put comic hysteria into history.'

He was also working for modern history, too—far away from the cameras. Back home in Ireland, he decided to organise a one-man election campaign for Michael Higgins when he stood for The Dail. Acknowledging widely Peter's help in getting him elected, Higgins then became Chairman of the Irish Republic's Labour Party.

Peter's love of Ireland wasn't limited to political activities, however. A new romance appeared to be blossoming with actress Karen Browne. And America had proved it wanted him when his own country was trying to bring back the bird. So he was acknowledging it by saying yes to their offers of employment. He started planning his next American film, a new version of *Svengali*. It was almost as if it were another example of that strange sense of loyalty that has guided much of the O'Toole career.

Svengali was an old story, updated. O'Toole was to play the singing teacher who provides a basically untalented girl—in this case played by Jodie Foster—with the voice of an angel, which she loses when he is not around. In the new version, which was intended for television and took nine months to film, the girl sings with a rock group.

By all accounts, Peter and Jodie, who was finding it hard to recover from being the target of the obsessions of President Ronald Reagan's would-be assassin, John Hinkley, got on beautifully—well enough to be photographed holding hands in the midst of the New York winter of early 1982. 'I don't remember when I laughed as much,' said nineteen-year-old Jodie.

In the autumn of 1982, he was going back to one of his most successful plays—Shaw's *Man and Superman* with which he knew he would be able to regain his old glories.

Peter's younger daughter, Pat, joined him in this come-back performance, playing a maid who had just one word to say: 'What?' It was the nearest either of the O'Toole daughters had ever come to being seen and not heard.

During the run of the play at Birmingham, Peter gate-crashed a party Pat gave for some of her young friends at the theatre. He was in a nightshirt which, she said, 'barely covered his buttocks'.

There was still the ever-present need to lay the ghost of *Macbeth,* which to some people's minds had replaced that of *Hamlet* as the most haunting apparition in the theatre. He said he thought it had been a 'marvellous experience' and didn't regret a moment of it. Was that really true? People who know Peter O'Toole well will say that what hurt him most was that it all reflected on his status as an actor, a calling he has always regarded as never less than sacred. If it had commercial advantages, they were merely secondary.

In fact, money has not been the guiding factor in his life. When he needed cash, it came from the Hollywood-backed films, and the amount they were offering had to be sufficient to meet not merely his requirements, but also his own assessment of his importance. There is no greater barometer to a performer's position on the totem pole than the number of noughts he can command on his pay cheque. And yet when a top publisher offered him £250,000 to write his autobiography, he turned it down flat. He was no more interested in the money than he was in telling his own story.

But he has been doing some serious writing. He has been working on a story of his grandmother's racing days. There is a novel in the works and a play, too—which he has not yet planned to produce but which, already, a group of his friends have started acting out at a series of private gatherings at the Connemara house.

And those friends have always been important to him. He can turn up at the apartment of someone like Leslie Bricusse who produced the score for *Mr Chips* and spend an hour or more reciting *Othello*. Or he and John Huston can simply sit in one of their houses in Ireland discussing films. 'We're very good friends, I'd say,' Huston told me. 'I like and admire him as both an actor and an individual. His sharpness, his quickness, his intelligence, his fine taste and literary judgment. He is a connoisseur.'

If he and Omar Sharif meet, it is usually a reunion that begins in the afternoon and ends the next morning. For once, talking about *Lawrence* is a time for happy memories and not anxiety.

Or he can see some of his old RADA buddies, like Alan Bates, whom he remembers meeting before he jumped on the wagon. Peter and Richard Burton were lying in the gutter after a surfeit of alcohol when Bates came along and pulled them both up on to their feet. 'Do you know Richard Burton?' Peter asked him. That is success of sorts.

Other friends like James Villiers say they wish they could just bump into him the way they used to be able to do—in the pubs of Hampstead. That they can't is perhaps success—certainly fame—of another sort.

He is a very complicated man. To some people, he remains an intimidating personality. Journalists have come back from sessions with him, saying that it was like a meeting with a head of state. They are either told to gather at a certain rendezvous from whence they will be conveyed to The

Presence, or else they go to his house and are told precisely where he will sit when he comes in to talk to them. From that stage on, all is fun, laughter and a considerable dose of O'Toole wit.

In Connemara, he is not so much the local celebrity, as the tall man who strides intently down the road from Frank Kelly's shop to the Abbeyglen Hotel, where he has been known to sit sipping a lemonade or eating a quiet, unpretentious meal.

He still lays off the hard stuff, although there are some friends who wonder whether the prodigious amounts of strong tea and coffee he consumes might not provide him with as much danger from caffeine poisoning.

He remains intensely loyal and friendly to the people he likes. There are neighbours of his in Eirephort Road, who speak of his great desire to be simply one of them. One middle-aged lady told me that when he discovered she lived near him, he invited himself into her house and said: 'Now what have you got to drink?' She showed him a bottle of cider and he gave a disappointed look. He wasn't sure that he approved of people doing voluntarily what he had done involuntarily. But he smiled, thanked her warmly and said he looked forward to seeing her again. Now he never misses an opportunity to stop and chat.

Younger women still delight in being seen in his company and he will not shy away from them if the mood takes him. 'I still enjoy the chase,' he says.

But there are many who are very close to him who say that what he would enjoy most would be the impossible—to have Sian come back to him. Accepting that it is impossible, he lives a life that seems a world away from the hellraising for which he has such an effervescent reputation.

In Hampstead, he is the perfect father, never sure what his two daughters will do. After Kate went to Dublin, Pat decided to finish her education in Paris. He says he is not sure whether they will follow their parents' lead and go into the theatre or become brain surgeons.

It would be difficult for a man like him, with his passion for Ireland and the theatre, not to fall victim every now and again to nostalgia. He drinks it in the way he used to imbibe whisky and Guinness. That is why, when he can, he makes pilgrimages round the racetracks of the Yorkshire dales where his grandmother and father had introduced him to the fact that horses did more than give people rides. Naturally, he cannot now resist the opportunity of a small flutter.

No one really doubts that his ambition is to be recognised as one of the Great Actors. It is a profession for which he has the utmost respect, a fact that comes through even when he speaks about it in less than respectful tones. 'Acting,' he says, 'is farting about in disguise.'

But another time, he will say that he is dedicated to bringing back the glory that the theatre had before people starting experimenting. 'The theatre is no place for tentative gropings. It is for certainty and conviction. Experiment enough is to get my bones out of the dressing room and on to the stage and see if it will work.'

It has worked many more times than it has failed. Two hundred roles have testified to the fact. It worked at RADA, at Bristol, at Stratford, in the flowing robes of *Lawrence of Arabia,* in *The Lion in Winter.*

The ambition to play King Lear still burns within him. Will he do it? Probably not until he can convince himself that there will be no repeat of the Battle of Waterloo Road. But he will doubtless risk it. 'An acting career isn't a stroll through the park. We all have our ups and downs,' he says.

If he does win through, then Lear's throne may well be the one that will make the Crown Prince king.

Index

233

236

Walsh, Father Leo 15
Ward, Simon 179
Warner Brothers 89, 93, 108, 132
Warner, Jack L. 89
Waterloo 116
Welles, Orson 91, 185
West, Timothy 195–199, 201–208, 212–215, 218, 221, 222
What's New Pussycat? 112
Wilder, Billy 117
Williams, John 144, 146
Wilson, Angus 42
Wilson, Sir Harold 114

Wilson, Judy 115
Wolfit, Sir Donald 78, 211, 221
Wyler, William 119
Wymark, Patrick 68

Yates, Peter 150–152
Yeats, Jack 95, 129
Yeats, W.B. 95
York, Susannah 135, 140
Yorkshire Evening News 18

Zulu 179
Zulu Dawn 179–180